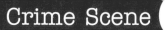
DNA Evidence

by Don Nardo

LUCENT BOOKS

An imprint of Thomson Gale, a part of The Thomson Corporation

THOMSON

GALE

Detroit • New York • San Francisco • New Haven, Conn. • Waterville, Maine • London

LIBRARY OF CONGRESS CATALOGING-IN-PUBLICATION DATA

Nardo, Don, 1947-
  DNA evidence / by Don Nardo.
     p. cm. -- (Crime scene investigations)
  Includes bibliographical references and index.
  ISBN 978-1-59018-951-1 (hardcover)
  1. DNA fingerprinting--Juvenile literature. 2. Forensic genetics--Juvenile literature. I. Title.
  RA1057.55.N37 2008
  614'.1--dc22
                        2007021910

ISBN-10: 1-59018-951-5
Printed in the United States of America

Contents

Foreword

The popularity of crime scene and investigative crime shows on television has come as a surprise to many who work in the field. The main surprise is the concept that crime scene analysts are the true crime solvers, when in truth, it takes dozens of people, doing many different jobs, to solve a crime. Often, the crime scene analyst's contribution is a small one. One Minnesota forensic scientist says that the public "has gotten the wrong idea. Because I work in a lab similar to the ones on *CSI*, people seem to think I'm solving crimes left and right—just me and my microscope. They don't believe me when I tell them that it's the investigators that are solving crimes, not me."

Crime scene analysts do have an important role to play, however. Science has rapidly added a whole new dimension to gathering and assessing evidence. Modern crime labs can match a hair of a murder suspect to one found on a murder victim, for example, or recover a latent fingerprint from a threatening letter, or use a powerful microscope to match tool marks made during the wiring of an explosive device to a tool in a suspect's possession.

Probably the most exciting of the forensic scientist's tools is DNA analysis. DNA can be found in just one drop of blood, a dribble of saliva on a toothbrush, or even the residue from a fingerprint. Some DNA analysis techniques enable scientists to tell with certainty, for example, whether a drop of blood on a suspect's shirt is that of a murder victim.

While these exciting techniques are now an essential part of many investigations, they cannot solve crimes alone. "DNA doesn't come with a name and address on it," says the Minnesota forensic scientist. "It's great if you have someone in custody to match the sample to, but otherwise, it doesn't help. That's the investigator's job. We can have all the great DNA evidence in the world, and without a suspect, it will just sit on the shelf. We've all seen cases with very little forensic evidence get solved by the resourcefulness of a detective."

While forensic specialists get the most media attention today, the work of detectives still forms the core of most criminal investigations. Their job, in many ways, has changed little over the years. Most cases are still solved through the persistence and determination of a criminal detective whose work may be anything but glamorous. Many cases require routine, even mind-numbing tasks. After the July 2005 bombings in London, for example, police officers sat in front of video players watching thousands of hours of closed-circuit television tape from security cameras throughout the city, and as a result were able to get the first images of the bombers.

The Lucent Books Crime Scene Investigations series explores the variety of ways crimes are solved. Titles cover particular crimes such as murder, specific cases such as the killing of three civil rights workers in Mississippi, or the role specialists such as medical examiners play in solving crimes. Each title in the series demonstrates the ways a crime may be solved, from the various applications of forensic science and technology to the reasoning of investigators. Sidebars examine both the limits and possibilities of the new technologies and present crime statistics, career information, and step-by-step explanations of scientific and legal processes.

The Crime Scene Investigations series strives to be both informative and realistic about how members of law enforcement—criminal investigators, forensic scientists, and others—solve crimes, for it is essential that student researchers understand that crime solving is rarely quick or easy. Many factors—from a detective's dogged pursuit of one tenuous lead to a suspect's careless mistakes to sheer luck to complex calculations computed in the lab—are all part of crime solving today.

In the Footsteps of Sherlock Holmes

Today, thanks to popular television shows like those in the *CSI* series, most people have at least a basic understanding of what DNA is and know that analysis of DNA can be used to solve crimes. DNA is a chemical found in genes, the genetic blueprints of humans and other living things. Shows like *CSI* constantly remind viewers that no two people have identical DNA. Indeed, each living thing has its own, unique genetic fingerprint. Therefore, matching traces of DNA found at a crime scene to the DNA of a suspect can help show that the suspect committed (or did not commit) the crime.

Modern television detective dramas have also shaped the public's perception that DNA fingerprinting is part of a special branch of science called forensic science, or "forensics" for short. Forensics applies scientific methods to legal matters, particularly to solving crimes. DNA is not the only form of forensic evidence used in the fascinating world of forensic science. The forensic experts depicted on *CSI* and other shows regularly supplement their DNA analysis by examining finger and palm prints, shoe and tire tracks, blood types, cloth fibers, and many other kinds of forensic evidence. In these shows, analyzing forensic evidence almost always leads to the capture and conviction of those who committed the crime.

Early Use of Science in Solving Crimes

As is often portrayed in television detective dramas, DNA analysis as a cutting-edge scientific technique that became available to law enforcement officials only in the last couple of decades. What the shows do *not* reveal is that the forensic use of DNA is the end product—in a way the pinnacle—of a long, winding, often uneven history of scientific crime solving. True, public knowledge of forensic methods did not exist until about a century ago. However, police and other government authorities have attempted to solve crimes throughout record-ed human history. And basic scientific techniques—although not yet called "science" or "forensics"—were introduced into the process a little at a time over the centuries.

The earliest known use of science to solve a crime involved the famous ancient Greek thinker Archimedes of Syracuse. The city's king, Hiero had a royal crown of pure gold made for him. But Hiero thought that the craftsman who had fash-ioned the crown might have cheated him. He suspected the man had secretly mixed a small amount of gold with quantities a cheaper metal. Archimedes proceeded to test the crown in order to confirm or deny Hiero's suspicion. The scientist con-ducted what is now seen as a classic experiment, based on the fact that a pound of silver takes up almost twice as much space as a pound of gold. Archimedes immersed the crown in water and saw that the amount of water displaced was consistent with a mixture of silver and gold, not pure gold. In this way, the "crown caper" was confirmed and the craftsman caught and punished.

Though scientifically based, Archimedes' feat did not involve a crime scene or a murder, often the meat of foren-sic cases. The first known use of forensics to solve a murder case occurred in China in medieval times. In 1248, a Chinese writer named Song Ci compiled a book titled *Collected Cases of Injustice Rectified*. It told about various investigations by doc-tors and other authorities into people's deaths to make sure that justice had been served. In one prominent case, a man had been murdered with a sickle. In an effort to find the guilty party, the investigator asked each villager who owned a sickle to bring it to him. After a while, flies began to congregate on one particular sickle. The investigator reasoned that the flies had been attracted to traces of blood left on the blade after

Greek scholar Archimedes was one of the first to use science to solve a crime.

the killer had wiped it off. The investigator was able to get a confession from the sickle's owner and thereby solve the murder. Today, an investigator would test the blade for traces of DNA and compare these to the DNA of the victim.

The Birth of the CSI

Centuries later, various other forensic techniques developed in Europe, especially in nineteenth-century France and England. In 1816, for example, a young woman who lived in Warwick, England, was murdered. A bright police investigator found boot prints and the impression of a certain kind of cloth in the soft earth near the body. He then matched these impressions with the boots and trousers of a farm laborer who lived nearby, solving the case. Another forensic technique developed after two French doctors, Paul Brouardel and Ambrose Tardieu, studied and catalogued the classic physical signs of murder on a human body, including typical signs of suffocation and strangulation. Unlike today's forensic scientists, Brouardel and Tardieu did not yet know that a murderer's DNA is often found in skin cells left behind on the rope used for the strangling.

Inspired by these and other early investigators, in the mid-1800s a young English physician named Alfred Swaine Taylor began teaching forensic medicine in London. He was the first researcher to advocate a careful examination of *all* evidence at a crime scene by a trained medical expert. In a way, this marked the birth of the modern CSI, or crime scene investigator. "A medical man, when he sees a dead body," Taylor wrote,

> should notice everything. He should observe everything which could throw a light on the production of wounds or other injuries found upon it. It should not be left to a policeman to say whether there were any marks of blood on the dress or on the hands of the deceased, or on the furniture of the room. The dress of the deceased, as well as the body, should always be closely examined by a medical man.[1]

Scottish mystery writer Sir Arthur Conan Doyle created fictional detective, Sherlock Holmes, whose forensic work, examining bodies and surveying crime scenes, captured the public's imagination.

One thing that these and other early forays into forensics had in common was that the general public was blissfully unaware of them. Only a few trained experts knew about and understood the principles advocated by Taylor. That state of affairs changed rather abruptly in the late 1800s, however, thanks to a talented Scottish mystery writer named Arthur Conan Doyle (1859–1930). Between 1887 and 1915, Doyle turned out several stories and books featuring his now immortal fictional detective, Sherlock Holmes. Doyle based the character on one of his college professors, Joseph Bell, who along with Taylor, was a pioneer of forensic science. In fact,

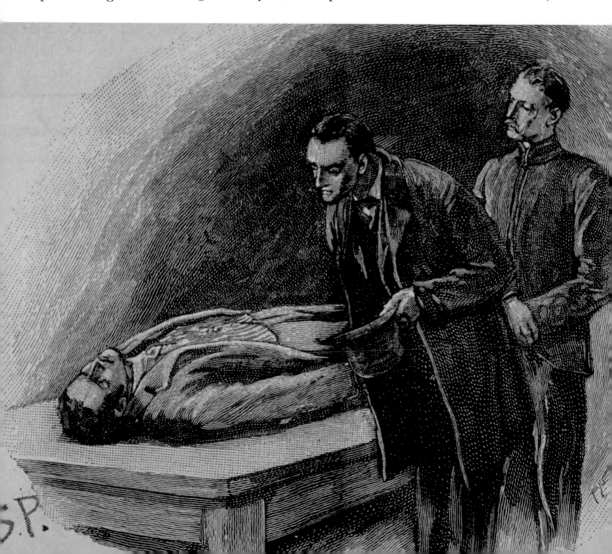

Bell often used the phrase "it was elementary" when describing a successful diagnosis. And Doyle often put those same words in Holmes's mouth in the stories.

Like Taylor, Bell, and other real forensic experts of that time, Holmes paid close attention to detailed evidence at crime scenes. In Doyle's *A Study in Scarlet*, for instance, Holmes's sidekick, Dr. Watson, says of Holmes: "His nimble fingers were flying here, there, and everywhere, feeling pressing, unbuttoning, examining [everything at the crime scene]."[2] In another of Doyle's tales, *The Adventure of Shoscombe Old Place*, Holmes examines evidence under a microscope and tells Watson:

> Have a look at these scattered objects [on the microscope slide]. Those hairs are threads from a tweed coat. The irregular gray masses are dust. There are epithelial scales [skin cells] on the left. Those brown blobs in the center are undoubtedly glue.[3]

Holmes's meticulous forensic detective work captured the public imagination of that and later generations. And in a way, all later CSIs and other forensic scientists followed in Holmes's footsteps. Because Doyle did not know of the existence of DNA, Holmes never used DNA analysis to solve crimes. In the 1950s, only a little more than two decades after Doyle's death, DNA was discovered. And in the 1980s, the technique of DNA fingerprinting was introduced, initiating the modern age of CSI.

The Piercing Sound of Truth

Most people did not know much about DNA and its use in solving crimes until the infamous O.J. Simpson case in the late 1990s. A former football star, Simpson was accused and eventually found innocent of murdering his ex-wife and her friend. Riveted to their television sets, millions of people watched the prosecutors and defense attorneys argue about forensic evidence, including DNA evidence. The first of the *CSI* television shows appeared shortly afterward, in 2000. The program producers hoped to tap into the increasing public awareness of and interest in forensics and DNA. *CSI* was hugely successful, becoming the highest-rated show on television and inspiring two very popular spinoffs, *CSI: Miami* and *CSI: New York*.

Today, largely as a result of these programs and other detective shows, the general public has a high level of confidence in DNA analysis to solve crime. According to real crime scene

Real vs. Television Forensic Labs

Forensic investigators and analysts who create DNA profiles are often asked how their work compares to that in depictions in TV shows such as *CSI*. One major difference the real CSIs cite is that in real crime investigations the investigators who collect evidence at crime scenes usually do not interview witnesses and chase down criminals. In most cases, neither do the investigators analyze the samples in the lab. That task is carried out by trained analysts who usually remain always in the lab. Another difference between the television shows and reality is that the shows depict the DNA analysis happening much faster and easier than it usually does in real life. Moreover, due to budgetary restraints, most real crime labs are understaffed and have large backlogs of work, making the solving of crimes even slower. Recognizing these realities, in May 2001, William Petersen, who portrays Gil Grissom on the original *CSI* show, appeared before the U.S. Congress and pleaded for more funding for the country's crime labs. "The 'CSI' lab processes evidence and solves crimes in a mere 44 minutes allotted to a network program," Petersen said. "But we all know that this is not the reality of the approximately 450 crime labs and coroner's labs across our country. Their reality is quite different than the manufactured world of my character and 'CSI.'"

Quoted in Robin Franzen, "TV's 'CSI' Crime Drama Makes It Look Too Easy," *Portland Oregonian*, December 10, 2002.

investigators, that confidence is sometimes a bit too enthusiastic. In truth, they point out, these shows sometimes glamorize forensics and exaggerate the capabilities and speed of DNA analysis and other forensic techniques. As one observer puts it, this gives many viewers "impossibly high expectations of how easily and conclusively criminal cases can be solved using DNA analysis and other forensic science."[4] Nevertheless, DNA evidence can be used to solve many crimes that otherwise might not have been solved. At the same time, it can clear innocent people who have been mistakenly convicted of crimes. In short, DNA analysis can in many circumstances be a shining path to the truth. In the words of former Manhattan Assistant District Attorney Harlan Levy, DNA evidence

> can avoid many miscarriages of justice that might occur without it, in a world where the truth is often hidden and elusive. . . . At long last, thousands of years after Cain killed Abel [the first murder, as described in the Bible], science has provided the means to hear blood cry out the names of those who have brought violence on others. It is a technology that must be nurtured and protected, for a society that treasures justice cannot afford to turn away from the piercing sound of truth.[5]

CHAPTER 1

Development of DNA Profiling

Until the 1980s, police detectives investigating crimes were limited to collecting, examining, and interpreting a limited range of evidence. They could collect and examine fingerprints, for instance, but not all criminals leave fingerprints. Also, fingerprints easily smudge, making them unreadable, and they wear away after a while (lasting a few years at best). In addition, only a small fraction of people in a given society have their fingerprints on record. So even when police are able to recover fingerprints from a crime scene, they sometimes have no way to make a match.

Investigators could also collect and examine blood samples from a crime scene, a technique called blood-typing. They might find some traces of type B-positive blood and some traces of type A-positive blood at a murder scene, for example. After taking a sample of the victim's blood and finding that it was B-positive, they could reasonably conclude that the A-positive blood came from the murderer. This was only partially helpful, however. First, hundreds of millions of people in the world have A-positive blood. So in theory, anyone with A-positive blood living in the area where the murder occurred might be the guilty party. Also, sometimes multiple blood samples at crime scenes get mixed together. If types A and B combine, it can often look like still another blood type—AB, making blood-typing in that case useless.

What crime investigators needed was a forensic technique that was far more precise and conclusive than either finger-printing or blood-typing. They needed a way to zero in on and firmly identify a culprit from among thousands of potential suspects. This is what they got when DNA profiling

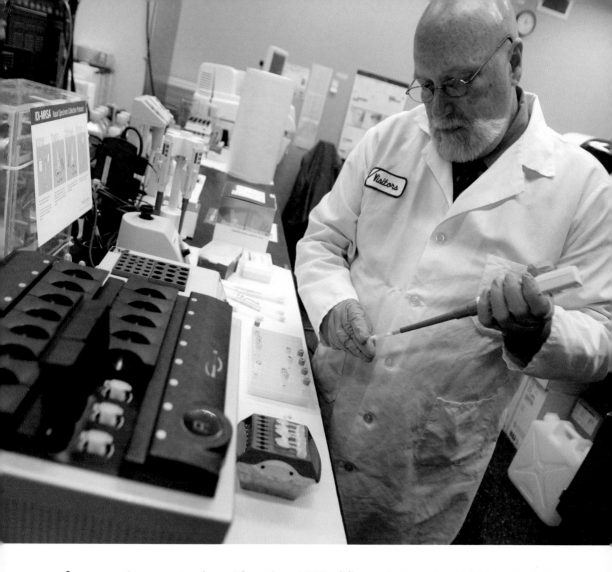

first came into use in the mid-to-late 1980s. The technique is also referred to as DNA fingerprinting, genetic fingerprinting, DNA analysis, DNA forensics, and DNA testing.

Whatever one chooses to call it, the use of DNA to solve crimes has revolutionized police work and legal systems in countries around the world. This is because of the special nature of DNA, a core part of the genetic blueprints of life. Because the DNA of everyone in the world is unique, one person's DNA, in theory, can be differentiated from the DNA of everyone else. That gives forensic scientists, police detectives, lawyers, and judges a far better chance of identifying murderers and other criminals with a high degree of certainty

DNA analysis is a forensic technique far more precise than either fingerprinting or blood-typing.

15

and making sure that these lawbreakers are punished. In a very real way, therefore, the discovery of DNA and its first applications to crime solving constitute one of the great triumphs of modern science. As noted former prosecutor Harlan Levy puts

Becoming a Forensic DNA Analyst

Job Description:
A Forensic DNA analysis works mostly in a forensics lab, where he or she performs DNA tests on biological material that police investigators submit to the lab. The analyst also interprets the results of the DNA tests.

Education:
DNA analysts are usually required to have a bachelor's or in some cases a master's degree in chemistry, biology, or forensic science.

Qualifications:
In addition to a college degree, in most cases a DNA analyst must have a minimum of six months experience doing DNA casework (collecting samples, and so on), and/or experience in handing all kinds of forensic materials.

Additional Information:
The DNA analyst must be prepared to give expert testimony in court when called on to do so. He or she must also be able to periodically check the reliability of lab equipment and procedures and to help train new analysts hired by the lab.

Salary:
$35,000-$65,000

it: "The story of the discovery of DNA analysis and [its] first use brings together science at its most wondrous and crime at its most heinous."[6]

The DNA Pioneers

The story of the development of DNA profiling actually began in 1952. That year, two American researchers, Alfred Hershey and Martha Chase, made an important discovery. Working in their Cold Spring Harbor Laboratory in Long Island, New York, the researchers studied a substance found in the bodies of all living things: dioxyribonucleic acid, or DNA for short. Between 1869 and 1950, a number of researchers around the world had isolated DNA and studied it. But no one was quite sure exactly what its purpose was. Until Hershey and Chase's breakthrough, the connection between DNA and heredity—the passing on of traits from one generation to the next—had not been made conclusively. The prevailing theory was that certain proteins controlled heredity. Hershey and Chase made that vital connection. They proved that DNA is a kind of genetic material carrying at least some of the blueprints of life.

American scientist James D. Watson, left, and English scientist Francis Crick were able to decipher the structure of DNA molecules.

But the manner in which DNA determines the genetic makeup of people and animals was still uncertain. This was because the structure of the DNA molecule remained a mystery. Hoping to solve this mystery, American scientist James D. Watson and English scientist Francis Crick began intensively studying DNA. In 1953, they announced their historic findings. What these DNA pioneers found was that the DNA of people and animals is stored in the nucleus, or center, of nearly every cell in the body. Also, DNA molecules are not only huge, as molecules go, but also uniquely shaped. Watson and Crick discovered that each DNA molecule consists of two long strands of genetic material. One strand comes from a person's mother and the other from his or her father. In that way, every person inherits some genetic information from each parent.

The Double Helix and Human Genome

Watson, Crick, and their colleagues also showed that the two strands inside each DNA molecule twist around each other, forming an elegant, winding spiral that scientists call a double helix. This double helix is also like a twisting ladder because the two strands are connected in thousands of places by little rungs. Each rung is composed of two parts, called nucleotide bases. Each grouping of two is called a base pair. In all, a typical DNA molecule has about three billion base pairs, for a total of some six billion bases.

These bases are almost always made up of the same four chemicals—guanine (G), cytosine (C), thymine (T), and adenine (A). The chemicals arrange themselves on the DNA ladder in varying patterns, called sequences. Such sequences can be short or long. One of the many short sequences is: AGCTCAATCG.

Put more simply, the chemical sequences that extend through the base pairs of a DNA molecule form small bits of genetic information. And each of these bits determines a single aspect of the complex blueprint for constructing the body of one person or animal. One bit of information, for example, might instruct the body to make a certain protein needed to form muscle tissue. Another bit might command the body to make blue eyes rather than brown ones. A piece or section of DNA that contains all the information needed for one such command is called a gene. Thus, each gene consists of a series of chemical sequences that exist alongside one another on the double helix and together they perform a single genetic task. The ability to understand and distinguish individual genes is essential in DNA profiling. Likewise, scientists must be able to recognize alleles. An allele is part of or an alternate form of a gene. Usually, two alleles, one contributed from each parent, exist in each gene.

All of the base pairs, chemical sequences, genes,

DNA molecules form a double helix, resembling a twisting ladder. The genes in each DNA molecule are essential for DNA profiling.

and alleles in the DNA of human beings add up to the genetic code, or blueprint of human life. There are also unique genetic blueprints for chimpanzees, dogs, mice, elephants, fish, and other living things. The complete human genetic code is the human genome.

The "Eureka" Moment

In the years following Watson and Crick's description of the DNA double helix, it became clear that close to 99.9 percent of the human genome is identical in all people. Therefore, only one tenth of one percent of the sequences, genes, and alleles are different. These differences are what distinguish one person from another. A tenth of one percent may not sound like much; however, it consists of some three million base pairs. And when sorted or arranged in different ways, these can produce billions or trillions of possible variations.

It was this tenth of a percent and its many potential variations that attracted the interest of the father of DNA profiling, Englishman Sir Alec Jeffreys. A geneticist, Jeffreys began working at a lab at the University of Leicester in 1977. In the years that followed, he and his colleagues studied genes and how they evolve and change. This invariably led him to look at sections of the DNA double helix that seemed to be different in different individuals—called areas of variability, or hypervariable regions. Within these areas are short chemical sequences that came to be called minisatellites.

Jeffreys searched for ways to probe and better observe these minisatellites. "We made a probe that should latch onto lots of these minisatellites at the same time," he explained. Then one day in September 1984, the researchers used an X-ray machine, like that used by dentists and doctors, to take a sort of picture of what the probe had revealed. Jeffreys recalled:

> I took one look [and] thought 'what a complicated mess.' Then suddenly [I] realized we had patterns. There was a level of individual specificity that was light

years beyond anything that had been seen before. It was a 'eureka!' moment. Standing in front of this picture in the darkroom, my life took a complete turn.[7]

A "eureka" moment is one in which a person suddenly sees clearly some great fact or truth that no one had ever thought of or found before. Jeffreys and his colleagues recognized that they had done more than create images of areas of DNA variability. In and of itself, that was certainly a difficult and important feat that would advance the course of modern science. But they also immediately realized that the patterns of minisatellites on the X-ray could be used in other areas of science, including forensic science. In particular, since these areas of

Geneticist Dr. Alec Jeffreys, creator of the DNA fingerprinting process, examines a DNA fingerprint.

DNA variability were different for each person, they could be used to distinguish one person from another. In a later interview, Jeffreys explained:

> The implications for individual identification [was] obvious. . . . It was clear that these hypervariable DNA patterns offered the promise of a truly individual-specific identification system. . . . For the first time [there was] a general method for getting at large numbers of highly variable regions of human DNA. Also, almost as an accidental by-product, it suggested approaches for not only developing genetic markers for medical genetic research, but for opening up the whole field of forensic DNA typing.[8]

The Father of DNA Analysis

Alec Jeffreys, the inventor of DNA analysis (or testing), was born on January 9, 1950, in Oxford, England. As a young man he attended the University of Oxford and in 1977 began working at the biological labs at the University of Leicester. It was at Leicester in 1984 that he was able to separate DNA fragments into recognizable patterns and record them using an X-ray machine. This process, called RFLP (restriction fragment length polymorphism), remained the standard method of DNA analysis for several years. Using RFLP, Jeffreys aided local police in solving the famous Colin Pitchfork case in the late 1980s. Having become a world-famous scientist, Jeffreys was elected to the prestigious scientific organization, the Royal Society, in 1986, and in 1994 the English queen knighted him, making him Sir Alec Jeffreys. He also won the Albert Einstein World Award of Science in 1996. In recent years, Jeffreys has been studying the effects of radiation on DNA.

Advantages of the New Technology

By "forensic DNA typing," Jeffreys meant a way of using DNA in the same way that detectives use fingerprints to seek out and arrest criminals. So he quickly coined the term "genetic fingerprinting," now more commonly called DNA profiling. The new technology seemed to possess a number of distinct and remarkable advantages for investigators trying to identify suspects in criminal cases. First, the chances of any two people having identical DNA, especially in the variable region of minisatellites, is extremely tiny. Therefore, a DNA test can produce a genetic snapshot that can single out one suspect from all other suspects. Former prosecutor Harlan Levy explains the eye-opening mathematical probabilities involved:

> It may be that a DNA fragment [group of minisatellites] in one sample that could be expected to occur in one person in 100 . . . matches a fragment in [another] sample. That is significant but hardly overwhelming. But if there is a DNA match at another location [on the DNA helix taken from the samples], the numbers suddenly grow exponentially [at a tremendous rate]. . . . The chances of the two DNA profiles matching randomly are one in 10,000. . . . If there is a match at a third location . . . the numbers would go to 1 million. And if there is a fourth match . . . it goes to one in [many millions].[9]

Similarly, if a suspect has seven, eight, or nine matches, the chances that he or she is not the culprit is one in hundreds of billions or even trillions. Since there are only six billion people on Earth, it is extremely likely that the suspect is the guilty party.

Jeffreys and his colleagues realized a second advantage of DNA profiling. Nearly every cell in the human body has DNA in its nucleus. This means that almost any cell from a suspect, such as a skin cell, hair cell, saliva cell, or urine cell, carries the suspect's genetic fingerprint. This vastly expands the diversity of trace evidence that might be found at a crime scene and thereby increases the likelihood of identifying the criminal. Trace evidence consists of evidence found only in small amounts. "Fingerprints come only from fingers," researcher N.E. Genge writes.

But DNA can be found in blood, in urine, in feces, in saliva, in some hair, in the shed skin cells found in a facecloth or toothbrush—even in the sweatband of a hat! A suspect doesn't have to bleed at the [crime] scene to leave DNA. Semen at rape scenes, saliva on the envelope of a ransom note, skin cells scraped onto a rope while tying a victim—all provide the opportunity for collection and analysis.[10]

A DNA test can provide a genetic snapshot that can single out one suspect from all others, since the chance of any two people having the same DNA sequence is extremely rare.

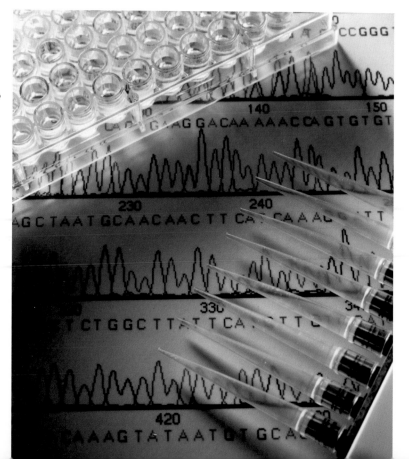

A third advantage of DNA collection and analysis is that DNA can survive longer than most other kinds of evidence. Most fingerprints smudge or disappear after a few weeks or months (although on occasion they can last a few years). In comparison, DNA can, under the right circumstances, last for centuries or even for millennia. Successful DNA analysis has been performed on Egyptian mummies three to four thousand years old, for example. And similar tests have been conducted, again successfully, on 25,000-year-old human remains found in a cave in southern Italy. Granted, it is too late to prosecute anyone for crimes committed in the dim past. However, the remarkable longevity of DNA evidence allows investigators to go back and look at so-called "cold cases." These are criminal cases five, ten, twenty, or even fifty years old that were never solved. If any evidence found at the crime scene is still in storage, it can be tested, and this could potentially solve the case. The culprit, if he or she is still alive, might be caught and jailed, or at least the victim's family can achieve some kind of closure.

By the Numbers

1 IN 1.7 QUADRILLION (MILLION BILLION): The odds of two people having an identical DNA profile.

Speaking of families, DNA's ability to indicate familial (family) relationships is still another advantage of the new technology. Because each person inherits some DNA from each parent, his or her DNA is very similar to, though not exactly the same as, that of the parents. A person's DNA is also similar to his or her siblings' DNA, and, to a lesser degree, to any aunts, uncles, and cousins.

A murder case that occurred in the Philippines illustrates how this can be helpful to crime investigators. Two people committed the murder, but only one was identified by an eyewitness and arrested. Some saliva found at the crime scene was analyzed, and the DNA it contained was very similar, but not an exact match, to the DNA of the man in custody. This

Pathologists inspect a 600-year-old mummy in a forensic laboratory. DNA can, under the right circumstances, last for centuries.

showed that the second killer was almost certainly one of this man's close relatives. Accordingly, police questioned the man's brother, who soon confessed to his role in the crime.

DNA's Promises Fulfilled

The case of the two Philippine brothers was not the first to use DNA samples to solve a murder. That distinction went to two related cases that occurred in England in the 1980s, in which Alec Jeffreys was instrumental in solving. The first murder took place in November 1983. A 15-year-old schoolgirl named Lynda Mann went missing in the village of Narborough, only six miles from where Jeffreys was hard at work in his lab.

The next morning, someone found the girl's body on a footpath in the local woods. The coroner (a doctor who specializes in examining dead bodies) determined that she had been strangled to death. There were also semen stains on her vagina and pubic hair, indicating that a rape or attempted rape had occurred. Unfortunately, no other evidence was found—no fingerprints, clothes fibers, or the like. The semen was all the police had to go on. But because DNA profiling did not yet exist, there was no way to tell whose semen it was. So the case could not be solved.

The situation was different, however, when three years later, in July 1986, another teenage girl was murdered in the same village. Two days after she was reported missing, police found the body of Dawn Ashworth. Like Mann, she had been strangled and raped. Police arrested a young man named George Howard, who worked at a nearby hospital. Witnesses had seen a man matching his description near the scene of the murder a few days before. At first, Howard denied any involvement in the crime. But under intense questioning, he finally confessed that he had raped and strangled Ashworth. The police now suspected that Howard had also killed Mann three years before. The methods and details of the two crimes were, after all, extremely similar. However, Howard steadfastly denied that he had committed the earlier crime.

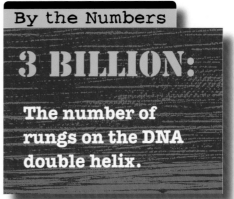

By the Numbers

3 BILLION:

The number of rungs on the DNA double helix.

Then, one of the detectives remembered reading about an important discovery called "genetic fingerprinting," that a local scientist had recently made. That scientist was Alec Jeffreys. Hoping for a break in the case, the police delivered a sample of the semen found on Mann and a sample of Howard's blood to Jeffreys. The geneticist gladly analyzed the DNA in both samples. What he found startled everyone. The DNA of Mann's killer did not match Howard's DNA, so Howard could not be the murderer in that case.

Even more surprising were the results when Jeffreys analyzed the semen found on Ashworth and compared its DNA to Howard's DNA. Again, there was no match. This meant that Howard had not killed either girl, and furthermore he had falsely confessed to the second murder! The police saw no other choice but to release him from custody. "I have no doubt whatsoever," Jeffreys later said, "that he would have been found

DNA samples examined by Dr. Alec Jeffreys were instrumental in solving a murder case in the 1980s. This was the first application of DNA in such a case and it was used to clear an innocent man and help convict the guilty one.

guilty had it not been for DNA evidence. That was a remarkable occurrence."[11]

The police were disappointed that they had to start from scratch in the two murder cases. But this time they were more confident because they were armed with the new DNA technology. Early in 1987 they began testing blood and semen samples from every man they could find in Narborough and surrounding villages. Detectives later found out that a local bakery worker, Colin Pitchfork, had paid another man to submit his own blood and claim it was Pitchfork's. The police arrested Pitchfork in September and he confessed to both murders. Dr. Jeffreys then administered new DNA tests to confirm the confession. The tests showed that Pitchfork's DNA exactly matched the DNA in the semen found on both dead girls.

By the Numbers

1 FOOT:

The length of each strand of DNA in each cell of a human or animal.

"It was an extraordinarily auspicious [fortunate or promising] beginning for the new [DNA] technology," Harlan Levy points out.

> In its first known application in a murder case, DNA testing fulfilled both its promises, clearing an innocent man and helping convict a guilty one. . . . DNA testing was completely new, but there was no doubt about its potential within the criminal justice system. Prosecutors and the press rushed to embrace the novel tool.[12]

Today that tool is a standard and vital one wielded by law enforcement officials across the United States and in many other nations.

CHAPTER 2

How DNA Profiling Works

The process of DNA profiling involves a number of consecutive steps, some of them complex and all of them requiring considerable skill and deliberate care. The skill comes from a lot of studying and training. Crime scene investigators and other experts who work with DNA samples must be highly educated and specially trained. With a few exceptions, these investigators and lab technicians have college degrees in biology, chemistry, genetics, forensic science, or some related scientific field. Moreover, some crime labs will only hire a DNA specialist who has a minimum of six months to a year of on-the-job experience.

Second, all through their education and training, these specialists are taught to be as careful as possible in handling samples at every step in the profiling process. This is because it is fairly easy to mishandle and contaminate a sample. And a contaminated sample is worthless, both to the police in cracking a case and in a court of law. Indeed, at times a DNA sample—perhaps from a hair or a bit of bodily fluid—is the key piece of evidence against a criminal suspect. If that evidence is contaminated, the law views it as compromised. The prosecutor will not be allowed to use it in court and the suspect may be set free, even if he or she is guilty. Conversely, contamination of a DNA sample might result in someone who was mistakenly sent to jail losing his or her only chance to be freed.

The steps in the DNA profiling process employed by these dedicated specialists can be conveniently grouped into two general categories. The first involves collecting the DNA evidence at the crime scene. The investigators follow strict guidelines designed to ensure that no evidence is missed and that any evidence found is properly handled. The second group of steps in the profiling process involves analyzing the samples in the lab. Again, the technicians who run the tests follow standard steps and guidelines developed over the past two decades and adopted by all professional forensic labs.

Kinds of DNA Evidence

In the first stage of DNA profiling, collecting the evidence, one or more trained investigators enter a crime scene. By this time, the police have set up boundaries (often using yellow tape) marking the extent of the crime scene. Usually, no one except police personnel is allowed inside these boundaries during the initial investigation. This helps to ensure that any evidence present, including DNA evidence, is not contaminated or otherwise compromised.

Remember that DNA evidence can, with a few exceptions, consist of almost any biological material from the human body. Important examples of such material are bodily fluids, including blood, saliva, urine, sweat, tears, and semen. In the case of blood, red blood cells have no nuclei and therefore do not contain nuclear DNA; however, white blood cells do contain

Swabs are one of the ways crime scene investigators collect DNA samples from evidence to analyze later in a lab.

Crime scene investigators strive to find hair samples with the hair root intact since it contains DNA, which can be used to identify a suspect.

nuclear DNA, so CSIs usually analyze the white blood cells. Other biological materials that originate inside the body, such as bones and teeth, also contain DNA. Among the other biological materials that might be found at a crime scene are those from the outer surfaces of the body. These include hairs and cells that were shed or scraped off. In the case of hairs, only the hair roots contain nuclear DNA, so investigators strive to find hair samples with the roots intact.

These various biological samples can be found in a number of places at a crime scene. Some are fairly obvious. Obvious places to look for saliva, for example, are the rims of cups and glasses, forks and other silverware, toothbrushes, telephone receivers, and cigarette butts. And the most common places investigators find semen specimens are the genital areas of rape victims, bed sheets, and discarded condoms. Likewise, skin cells from violent criminals are often found under the fingernails of victims who scratched them while resisting. And traces of incriminating blood are frequently discovered in the cracks between floorboards after a criminal has tried to clean up a crime scene.

In contrast, DNA evidence can turn up in places that are far less obvious and at times even surprising to untrained observers. For instance, valuable biological evidence can sometimes be found in the bathroom trash. A wastebasket can contain discarded tissues, cotton swabs, and other items containing traces of bodily cells or fluids. Similarly, contact lenses are typically coated with the wearer's tears, and envelopes that someone once licked might still contain traces of that person's saliva.

Still another example of the need to look in unexpected places for DNA evidence is urine. It might seem logical that urine samples would most likely be found in the bathroom, especially in, on, or around the toilet. Although this *is* often the case, experienced CSIs know that they should also look elsewhere, especially when the crime scene is in a natural setting. According to one veteran investigator who collected DNA at crime scenes for eighteen years:

After working a bunch of crimes that took us to cabins and other woodsy locations, we eventually came to the conclusion that, if you put ten guys in the woods and they've got to urinate, nine of those ten guys will prefer to pee on a tree trunk. Now, I'm sure that there's no manual to manhood that says you should pee on a tree . . . but you shine a source light around a campsite and I'll guarantee you there'll be DNA from urine on some tree somewhere [in the area].[13]

Cat Hairs Catch a Killer

Humans are not the only animals that possess DNA. In fact, all animals have DNA, and the DNA of all mammals is relatively similar in many ways to human DNA. Moreover, just as traces of human DNA can help solve crimes, so can traces of animal DNA. Forensic science researcher N.E. Genge tells about such a case:

One of the first cases linking two people through nonhuman DNA was investigated by the Royal Canadian Mounted Police (RCMP). While investigating a death in Prince Edward Island, examiners recovered two white hairs, which were at first thought to be those of the victim's ex-husband. They weren't. They were cat hairs. Not having a unit that dealt with cat DNA, the RCMP sent the hairs, as well as a blood sample from the ex-husband's white cat, to the National Cancer Institute's Cat Genome Project in Maryland. The lab there confirmed that both blood and fur came from the same cat, and the ex-husband was convicted of murder.

N.E. Genge, *The Forensic Casebook: The Science of Crime Scene Investigation.* New York: Ballantine, 2002, p. 150.

The Collection Process

It is important to emphasize that, at first, the investigator does not know which items and materials found at the crime scene are going to produce DNA evidence that will solve the crime. He or she might find a used napkin or some hairs, for example. But it might turn out that these belonged to the victim or an innocent bystander, not the suspect.

For this reason, the guidelines for evidence collection require that a wide range of items and biological materials be collected at the crime scene. These can be sorted through and analyzed later at the lab to determine their importance, or lack thereof, to the case. The U.S. National Institute of Justice (a division of the U.S. Department of Justice, in Washington, DC) issues a checklist of DNA-related items and materials that investigators should look for at a crime scene. The list includes, for example: fingernails, paper towels, tissues, Q-tips, toothpicks, straws, cigarette butts, blankets, sheets, mattresses, pillows, dirty laundry, eyeglasses, contact lenses, cellular phones, ropes, stamped envelopes, and used condoms.

Technicians follow careful guidelines to analyze samples in a lab, wearing gloves and sometimes masks that are changed often.

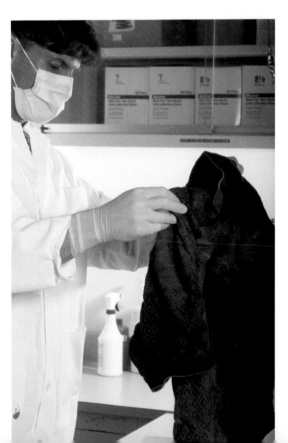

According to the collection guidelines, investigator should make sure not to touch any of the evidence with their bare hands or fingers. This is to keep an investigator's own cells and fluids from contaminating the evidence. The person doing the collecting should wear rubber gloves (like those worn by doctors during operations) and change them often. Also to avoid contamination, investigators should be careful not to touch their face, hair, glasses, and so forth while wearing the gloves.

In addition to the gloves, when possible, investigators are expected to use clean disposable items, such as cotton swabs, small wooden sticks, or wooden tweezers, to pick up the evidence. After picking up some evidence with a swab, for instance, an investigator always uses a new swab to pick up the next piece of evidence. That way, one piece of evidence does not contaminate another.

Having picked up the evidence, the investigator places it in a clean evidence bag, on a clean piece of paper or sterile tissue which is then rolled up, or in a glass test tube. Whatever container is used, it must be clearly labeled, saying what the

Wearing surgical masks in a forensic lab can help prevent against the possibility of saliva droplets landing on and contaminating evidence.

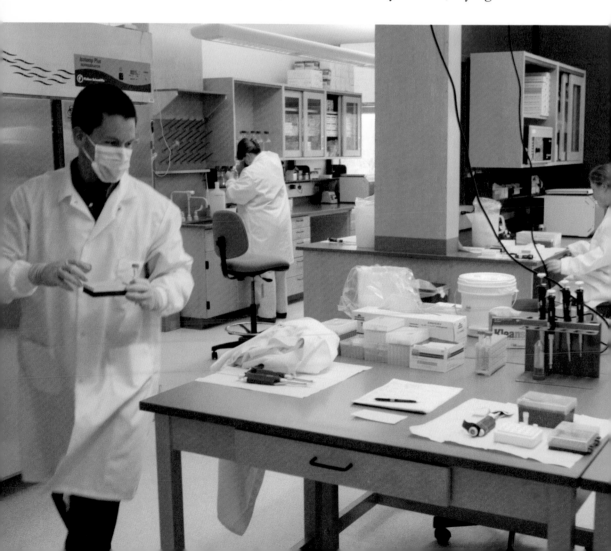

evidence is and where it was found. That helps eliminate mistakes later in the lab, such as accidentally mixing up two or more pieces of evidence.

Guidelines recommend that while handling and packaging evidence, investigators should refrain from sneezing, coughing, and, when possible, even talking. All of these activities spray tiny, largely invisible saliva droplets that can land on and contaminate the evidence. For this reason, many investigators wear surgical masks while handling evidence at a crime scene.

Conversely, the investigators and lab technicians need to be careful not to contaminate *themselves* with evidence that might cause them harm. Crime scene investigators, N.E. Genge points out, can come "into proximity with any number of bodily fluids" that could be carrying disease germs. "Biohazards like hepatitis and HIV are real dangers to investigators and laboratory personnel who handle bio-wastes and bio-fluids, so all samples must be treated as infectious until proven otherwise."[14]

In the Forensics Lab

All the evidence samples found and collected at the crime scene go immediately to the nearest forensics lab. The first step is evaluating the evidence. That is, the technicians must make sure that all the evidence is biological material that has the potential of containing DNA. Quite often the identity of various forms of evidence found at a crime scene is obvious. For example, a pool of dark red liquid lying beside a bullet hole or gash in a dead person's head is presumed to be blood. And yellowish stains found on the rim of a toilet seat are presumed to be urine.

However, investigators cannot always be sure what a substance really is until it is tested in the lab. In rare cases, for instance, a yellow stain on a toilet could be residue of some non-biological liquid that someone spilled there. Similarly, hairs found at a crime scene might have neither human nor animal origins; instead, they might be synthetic fibers from a wig. Whenever there is some doubt as to what a substance is, the lab technicians first run a brief preliminary test to identify it. This can save both time and money. Forensic DNA experts Norah Rudin and Keith Inman note that "It would be wasteful to run a full spectrum of DNA tests only to find no result because ketchup or shoe polish was analyzed."[15]

Once all the evidence samples are satisfactorily identified, it is time to test them for DNA. To make this possible, the DNA must be extracted, or separated from, the cells of the blood, semen, hair roots, bone marrow, or other biological

DNA Extraction

Extracting DNA from cells in a biological sample involves following these standard steps:

1 Lab technicians examine the sample, either through a microscope or through chemical testing, to make sure it really is biological in origin.

2 The confirmed biological sample, such as a piece of tissue or splotch of blood, is placed in glass test tube.

3 The lab technician adds some specialized chemicals. One of these, called a buffer, keeps the DNA molecules from disintegrating. The other chemicals break down the cells, allowing the DNA to separate out.

4 The technician divides the separated DNA into several small samples, each about the same size.

5 One of the DNA samples is frozen for possible use later. The rest is ready to undergo DNA analysis (or profiling).

Large DNA repositories allow labs to study DNA samples months or years later if a criminal investigation requires it.

material involved. The extraction process is fairly simple and usually takes less than an hour. The technician places the evidence sample in a small test tube and then pours in a few drops of some specialized chemicals. Some of these chemicals break down the cells and release the DNA molecules. Another chemical prevents these large molecules from falling apart, which can happen when they are exposed to the harsh world outside of the cell nucleus.

Having extracted the DNA, the technician separates it into two, three, or more separate samples. Most of these will be used for analysis. Usually one sample is stored in a freezer. That way the lab can study it months or years later if, for legal or technical reasons, the criminal investigation requires it.

The Other DNA

When people mention DNA and DNA analysis, they usually make reference to the principal source of DNA in the body, that found in the nuclei of cells. However, a second form of DNA also exists in other parts of each cell. Called mitochondrial DNA, abbreviated mtDNA, it is passed only from mother to child. For that reason, mtDNA does not change from generation to generation (except in the case of mutations). DNA analysis using mtDNA is performed fairly infrequently in most forensics labs. First, mtDNA analysis is far more expensive and time-consuming than testing that uses nuclear DNA. Also, by itself, mtDNA is not often useful in creating unique genetic profiles, mainly because nearly everyone in a given family has identical mtDNA. Still, mtDNA can be useful for ruling out certain suspects. In the famous Boston Strangler case from the 1960s, a man named Albert DeSalvo was suspected of being the culprit. Though he was not convicted, he did go to jail for other crimes and died in prison in 1973. Many years later, mtDNA taken from one of the victims was compared to mtDNA from the blood of DeSalvo's living brother. It did not match, proving that Albert DeSalvo was not the infamous strangler.

Initial Analysis of DNA Samples

Several different methods have been and continue to be used to analyze extracted DNA samples. The oldest method, introduced by Alec Jeffreys in the 1980s and still occasionally used, is known as RFLP (short for restriction fragment length polymorphism). RFLP uses a chemical substance called an enzyme to, in a sense, cut the very long DNA strands into a number of shorter pieces. These pieces tend to vary in length, from quite short to fairly long.

A scientist examines DNA sequencing. These films are often what are seen in court to give a visual representation of two matching sequences of DNA.

At this point, the DNA fragments remain mixed together in a disorganized jumble and are impossible to decipher. To impose some order on the fragments, the technicians place them in a special gel and run an electrical current through the gel. The current causes the fragments to move, and the distance they move within the gel depends on their weight. The smaller fragments move the farthest, in the process separating themselves from the heavier fragments. Eventually the separated fragments form distinct band-like patterns. When X-rayed, "these bands become visible," Genge explains.

> It's usually these films that are seen in court. If [the fragments in] two samples come from the same person, they'll break along the same lines and come to rest in the same places. That makes a match. If they aren't in the same place, there's no match. If there are considerable similarities but no match, it's possible the samples are from related individuals.[16]

RFLP analysis has long proven accurate and reliable. However, it does have some disadvantages. First, it is slow, requiring at least a few weeks to produce satisfactory results, which can be frustrating to police trying to crack a case in a timely fashion. Also, RFLP requires very large samples of DNA. Indeed, sometimes there is not enough DNA found at the crime scene to complete the analysis. In other situations, all of the DNA found must be used to complete the test, leaving none for storage.

PCR and STR to the Rescue

To overcome these shortcomings of RFLP analysis, scientists searched for ways both to increase the amount of DNA in samples and decrease the amount of time needed for analysis. A huge breakthrough occurred in the late 1980s. American biochemist Kary B. Mullis invented a new technique called PCR (short for polymerase chain reaction), for which he was awarded the Nobel Prize in chemistry in 1993. With the advent of PCR, forensic experts gained the ability to transform a tiny amount of DNA into a much larger, more workable sample.

PCR, sometimes called DNA amplification, increases the amount of DNA in a sample by replicating it on the chemical level. The technician places a small number of DNA fragments in a container and adds a special enzyme known as DNA polymerase. Using the A, C, G, and T bases in the DNA as, in a sense, raw materials, the enzyme stimulates the DNA fragments to reproduce themselves. When the amount of DNA in the sample has doubled, the process can be repeated, producing four times as much DNA as there was in the initial sample. In this manner, the technician can create as much DNA as he or she wants.

PCR has several benefits, the first of which is that it works very fast. A batch of DNA can be duplicated in only two or three minutes and within four hours or so a technician can increase the size of the initial sample by fifty times or more. PCR is also relatively inexpensive to perform. And it can successfully replicate very small samples of DNA that, due to exposure to the elements, have degraded in quality over many years.

A scientist collects DNA after a PCR (polymerase chain reaction), which allows forensic experts to transform tiny amounts of DNA into larger samples.

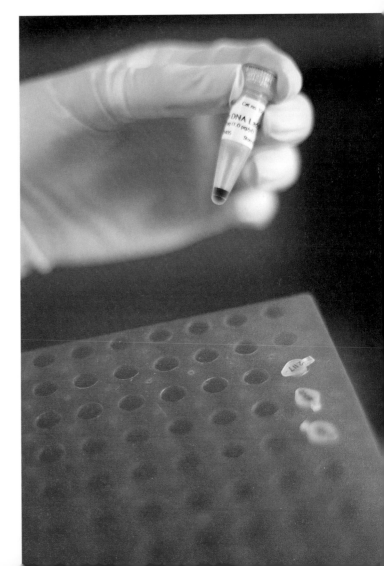

Lab technicians test the quality of a DNA sample with a DNA LabChip. STR allows CSIs to provide DNA profiles for samples that have severely degraded in quality.

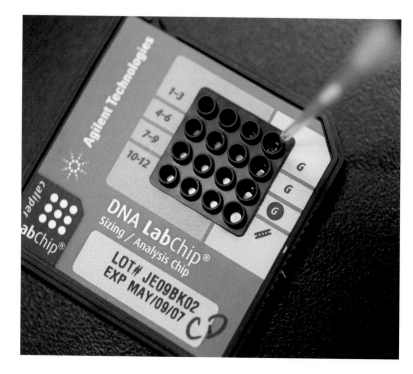

Another major breakthrough occurred in the mid-1990s with the introduction of a new method of DNA analysis—STR, which stands for short tandem repeats. As the term *tandem repeats* suggests, STR works by zeroing in on those sections of a DNA sample in which short sequences of base pairs repeat several times. For instance, in one person's DNA, there may be places where the sequence AATG repeats six times. In another person this sequence may repeat only four times. By examining these areas of repetition, scientists can easily determine that the DNA of the first person is different from the second person's DNA. Used in conjunction with PCR, STR quickly became the most often performed DNA profiling method in most forensics labs.

One significant advantage of STR analysis is that it works fairly quickly, especially when compared to RFLP analysis. Using STR, an experienced lab technician can create a DNA profile in about five or six hours. Another advantage of STR is that the short chemical sequences it utilizes are very stable.

The STR process

STR (short tandem repeats), at present the most commonly used method of DNA analysis, works in the following manner:

1 At a crime scene, an investigator collects what might be biological evidence, including such items as hairs, blood, skin cells, saliva, and so on.

2 At the lab, a technician first determines that the samples are indeed biological. Then he or she extracts DNA from the samples using various chemicals.

3 In many cases the technician finds that the amount of DNA is too small to analyze properly. So he or she employs PCR (polymerase chain reaction), a process that uses a chemical to create extra DNA identical to that in the sample. During PCR, fluorescent dyes are often mixed into the sample to make the DNA stand out from the liquid in which it is suspended.

4 The DNA is placed in a specialized gel, and in a procedure called gel electrophoresis, an electrical current is passed through the gel. This separates the DNA into fragments of varying length, with the shorter fragments appearing in the bottom part of the gel.

5 The technician uses a laser beam to scan a snapshot of the gel into a computer.

6 The computer recognizes and analyzes the repeated sequences of base pairs in the DNA and produces a visual image of its unique profile. That profile can now be compared to that of a suspect or to many profiles collected in a DNA database.

In fact, when exposed to the elements and other adverse conditions, these sequences can remain stable longer than entire DNA molecules can. Therefore, STR often allows CSIs to produce DNA profiles for badly decayed bodies in which most DNA molecules have partially deteriorated.

DNA Databases

Both PCR and STR have become increasingly reliable and standardized in recent years. One reason is the availability of commercial kits designed for use by forensic professionals. Each kit contains all the chemicals and other items needed to conduct the PCR and/or STR processes. Such kits have become a valuable tool in DNA profiling and its use in the conviction of criminals.

Another potent tool that DNA labs use to solve crimes consists of a series of computerized databases. These are electronic collections of DNA profile information that can easily be called up and viewed on a monitor. Each forensics labs keeps careful records of its DNA profiles and submits them to databases containing thousands of such profiles from many labs.

Individual U.S. states also have such databases. In addition, all fifty states are now required to submit the DNA information in their databases to a federal (national) database—the Combined DNA Index System, called CODIS for short. CODIS began as a pilot program in 1990 and became fully operational in 1998. The benefit of CODIS is that DNA profiles of criminals from across the country are all stored in one place. A forensics lab in any town in the nation can tap into the system at any time. If the technicians at a lab have developed a DNA profile but cannot find a suspect to match it, they can enter that profile into CODIS. The system then compares the profile to those already compiled. The profile of a

By the Numbers

3,977,433:

As of 2006, the number of DNA profiles of convicted offenders contained in the CODIS database.

person who earlier committed a crime in another state might be a perfect match for the lab's current profile. If so, the police have a real suspect to track down. According to CODIS's official Web site:

> Matches made among profiles in the Forensic Index can link crime scenes together, possibly identifying serial offenders. Based on a match, police in multiple jurisdictions can coordinate their respective investigations, and share the leads they developed independently. . . . After CODIS identifies a potential match, qualified DNA analysts in the laboratories contact each other to validate or refute the match.[17]

DNA data output from forensic equipment is input into federal databases that can be used in crime labs all over the country.

By December 2006, CODIS contained more than four million DNA profiles and had assisted in some forty-three thousand criminal investigations. These statistics confirm that the national database is one of the most comprehensive and successful scientific tools ever invented.

Indeed, the ability of CODIS and other computer databases to sort through DNA profiles and solve crimes has been proven repeatedly in the last decade. One of the most dramatic cases occurred in Ohio in 1993. A young woman in Cincinnati was raped by a man who broke into her apartment and held her at knifepoint. Investigators discovered ample biological evidence at the crime scene and were able to put together a DNA profile of the attacker. However, the Cincinnati police were unable to find any suspects who matched the profile.

Ten years passed without a break in the case. Then in 2003, Ohio created a database designed to compare DNA profiles of some inmates in the state's prisons to profiles in unsolved cases. In short order, the new database found a match. The profile of an inmate then serving time for burglary was identical to the profile the Cincinnati forensics lab had produced in the 1993 rape case. The inmate, Rodney J. Crooks, was about to be released after serving seven years for the burglary charge. Upon his release, the Cincinnati police arrested him for the 1993 rape. The DNA evidence was more than sufficient to send him back to prison. This and other cases like it demonstrate how modern forensics labs increasingly use rapidly advancing technology to hunt down, identify, and lock up individuals who pose a danger to society.

By the Numbers

41,900: As of 2006, the approximate number of positive hits made on the CODIS database by forensics labs.

CHAPTER 3

Classic Cases of DNA Profiling

DNA profiling has been and continues to be used in a wide variety of crime-related situations and cases. Among these, two kinds of cases are by far the most common. In the first, DNA evidence ends up proving that someone committed a crime and that person is convicted and punished. In the second broad category, DNA evidence proves that someone suspected or already convicted of a crime is actually innocent and that person gains his or her freedom. This second process is called exoneration, and someone cleared in such a manner is said to have been exonerated of guilt. Moreover, in a few criminal cases DNA has simultaneously convicted a guilty party and exonerated an innocent one. In the celebrated first use of DNA evidence to solve a crime, for example, Colin Pitchfork was convicted of two rape-murders and George Howard was cleared as a suspect in the same crimes.

Some convictions and exonerations brought about by DNA evidence have been fairly straightforward and clear-cut. Others have been more complex, with surprising twists and turns. What nearly all of these cases have in common is the extraordinary power of DNA profiling to demonstrate, with great accuracy, either guilt or innocence. That power is repeatedly revealed in the following classic cases.

DNA Profiling Reaches the United States

The case involving Howard and Pitchfork, which took place in England in the 1980s, sent shock waves through the criminal justice systems of many nations across the globe. And police departments far and wide were eager to learn how to

In older cases, a dead body can be exhumed and tested for DNA to exonerate, or prove the innocence of, someone.

use the exciting new DNA profiling technology. It was inevitable, therefore, that DNA analysis would soon begin solving crimes far removed from the English lab in which Alec Jeffreys invented it.

The first case in the United States that utilized DNA profiling was that of Tommy Lee Andrews. This case illustrates perhaps the most common and straightforward use of the technology: to confirm that a person already suspected of committing a crime is indeed guilty of that crime. The setting was Orlando, Florida, in 1986. That year the Orlando police investigated more than twenty cases with the same MO (from the Latin *modus operandi*), or pattern of behavior. In each case, a person began by prowling around a woman's home, peeping in the windows, and observing her daily routines. This typically went on for a week or more. Then the culprit broke into the home and sexually assaulted the woman. Eventually, a man named Tommy Lee Andrews was arrested because his face matched portraits in composite sketches. These drawings were made by a police artist based on the recollections of several of the victims.

Tommy Lee Andrews may well have been convicted solely on the women's eyewitness identifications. But the prosecuting attorney wanted to make his case as airtight as possible. And it so happened that he had recently read about a new company in Stamford, Connecticut, Lifecodes Corp., that was using DNA to help solve crimes. Intrigued, the prosecutor gathered up some biological evidence from the Orlando crime scenes and sent it to Lifecodes. The tests the company performed confirmed that Tommy Lee Andrews was indeed the person who had assaulted the Orlando women.

The Andrews case and other early similar cases involving DNA evidence gave American police and prosecutors a potent new tool to use in solving cases. And many existing forensics labs in the country quickly equipped themselves with the new technology. As a result, as time went on it became increasingly difficult for criminals in certain situations to deny their guilt.

The most common and straightforward use of DNA profiling technology is to confirm that a person already suspected of committing a crime is indeed guilty.

A clear example of this occurred in 2003. Before the advent of DNA profiling, police might suspect that someone had committed a murder. But more often than not, that suspect steadfastly denied committing the crime. And the existing evidence was not strong enough to convince a jury that the suspect was guilty beyond the shadow of a doubt. Such was the case of 16-year-old Sarah Johnson, daughter of Alan and Diane Johnson, prominent residents of Bellevue, Idaho. On September 2, 2003, the elder Johnsons were shot to death in their home. Some of the detectives working on the case found out that the deceased couple did not like Sarah's boyfriend, an illegal Mexican immigrant. It seemed possible that the Johnsons were planning to turn in the young man to

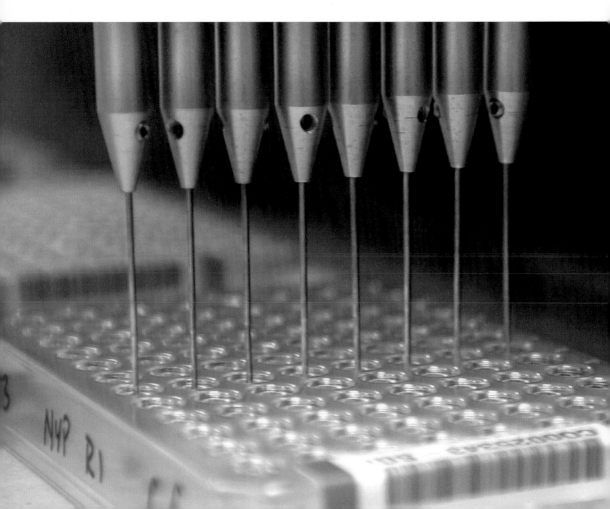

When DNA Does Not Convict

Using DNA evidence in a criminal case does not always ensure that the person charged with the crime will be convicted. A famous example was the O.J. Simpson case in 1995. The former football star was charged with killing his former wife, Nicole Brown Simpson, and her friend, Ronald Goldman. The prosecution presented DNA evidence taken from blood samples found on a sock and glove at the crime scene. And the prosecutors contended that the DNA evidence showed that the odds that Simpson was innocent were one in 170 million. Nevertheless, the jury found Simpson innocent. First, the jurors felt that the defense had successfully raised certain doubts about the defendant's guilt (including the fact that the bloodied glove did not fit Simpson's hand). Also, several jurors later admitted that they did not fully understand the meaning of the DNA evidence.

immigration authorities, and that might have been a motive for Sarah to kill her parents. However, though she admitted to being home at the time of the murders, she claimed she had nothing to do with them.

Sarah's claims of innocence were shown to be lies during the trial when the prosecutors introduced some incriminating DNA evidence. Police had found various blood-covered items, including a rubber glove, in a family trash barrel. And a DNA profile provided unmistakable scientific evidence against Sarah. Testifying on the witness stand, Cynthia Hall, a DNA analyst with the Idaho State Police, said, "The DNA profile obtained from the latex glove matched the profile obtained from the blood sample said to belong to Sarah Johnson."[18] Sarah Johnson was found guilty in 2005 and ordered to serve two life sentences without possibility of parole.

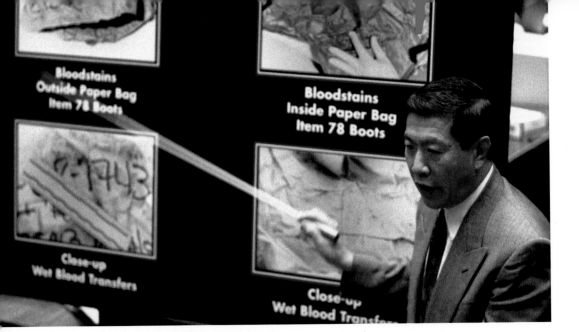

Bloodstains
Outside Paper Bag
Item 78 Boots

Bloodstains
Inside Paper Bag
Item 78 Boots

Close-up
Wet Blood Transfers

Close-up
Wet Blood Transfers

A forensic scientist gives testimony during the O. J. Simpson trial, where in spite of DNA evidence the former football star was acquitted of murder.

The Strange Case of Identical Suspects

As cases involving DNA profiling go, those of Tommy Lee Andrews and Sarah Johnson were fairly uncomplicated and unambiguous. The police had suspicions that a certain person was guilty and the DNA evidence merely confirmed that guilt. A good many other cases involving convictions obtained by DNA evidence have been far less simple and straightforward, however. Some have involved more than one suspect, for instance. And in a few, two suspects looked almost exactly alike, and DNA analysis was required to prove which was the guilty party.

One such case occurred in 1987 in the San Francisco Bay area. During the spring and summer of that year, two local women suffered brutal sexual assaults. Each described her attacker as a young, thin Hispanic male about 5 feet 7 inches tall. This naturally made the police suspect that the same man committed both assaults. That suspicion became even stronger when each victim helped a separate police artist prepare a sketch of the assailant. The two sketches were nearly identical.

Based on the sketches, police arrested a young Hispanic man and placed him in a traditional lineup. The first female victim immediately picked him out of the lineup and seemed certain he was the man who had attacked her. Fortunately for this suspect, though, DNA profiling had recently become available. His defense lawyer asked that his client's DNA be compared to that in the biological evidence found on the victims. The test showed that the suspect's DNA was not a match in either case. So the police felt they had no other choice but to let the suspect go.

While clearing the initial suspect, the DNA analysis had indicated that whoever had attacked the first victim had also attacked the second. The police now realized that the culprit must be a dead ringer for the initial suspect. At first, they were unable to find another man matching that description. But two years later they caught a break when a third woman was sexually assaulted in the same area. This time, police were able to make a quick arrest. And sure enough, the man in custody, Armando Quintanilla, looked exactly like both the initial suspect and the artists' sketches. Both men even had the same hairstyle and bushy mustache. When the local forensics lab produced a DNA profile of Quintanilla, it placed him at the

Many criminal cases involving rape and murder have been successfully linked together and prosecuted by comparing DNA charts.

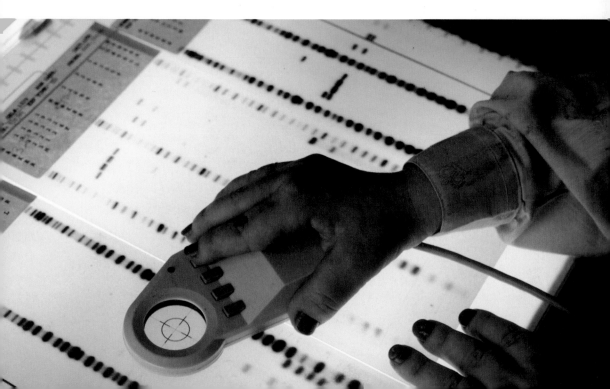

scene of all three assaults. This was more than enough proof for a conviction, and he was sentenced to life in prison.

Contradicting Victims' Testimony

One of the most striking aspects of the Quintanilla case was that DNA evidence ended up contradicting the eyewitness testimony of the first victim. She had been sure that the man she saw in the lineup was her assailant. But DNA evidence proved she was mistaken. In fact, police across the United States and in other countries sometimes find that eyewitness, including victims, can make incorrect identifications of their attackers. And thanks to the advent of DNA profiling technology, at least some of these mistakes can be rectified, saving innocent people from going to jail.

One of the most dramatic cases in which DNA performed this function was that of Carol Sanders and Gregory Ritter, both residents of Baltimore, Maryland. On August 16, 1990, Sanders, a single mother with a 7-year-old daughter, was sleeping on her living room couch. Suddenly, she was awakened by the sensation of someone's weight on top of her. At the same time, the intruder slipped a pillowcase over her head, so she was unable to see her attacker. Sanders tried to fight back but the man was very strong. He punched her repeatedly and proceeded to rape her, after which he fled the scene.

After calling 911, Sanders told the police that she was sure that the rapist was her former boyfriend, John Davis. The two had not been on good terms in recent months. And Sanders claimed that when the two had been a couple, Davis had occasionally displayed abusive behavior when he was angry. In addition, Sanders said she recognized Davis by the way he kissed her while raping her. Based on this strong testimony by the victim, the police

By the Numbers

184:

As of 2006, the number of people in the U.S. convicted of serious crimes and later exonerated by DNA evidence.

arrested Davis. However, he strongly denied committing the crime. Moreover, a DNA test was performed, and it backed up his story. Davis's DNA did not match the DNA sample from the semen investigators had collected at the crime scene.

As it turned out, Davis helped the police catch the real rapist. He told them that while he was in jail immediately after his arrest, he recognized and spoke to one of the other prisoners. That man, Gregory Ritter, had been the boyfriend of one of Carol Sanders' girlfriends. Davis remembered that when he told Ritter he had been arrested for raping Sanders, Ritter got an odd look on his face. Based on this lead, the police began investigating Ritter. And as time went on, the detective assigned to the case, Terry Woodhouse, increasingly felt that they now had the right man. As attorney Harlan Levy tells it:

DNA samples extracted in a lab can sometimes contradict eyewitness testimony and be the sole factor exonerating or convicting the suspect.

Ritter fit the description Sanders had given of her attacker better than Davis. Ritter's police photo also showed a substantial amount of hair on his chest sticking

out from the top of his shirt. When Carol Sanders had described her assailant to the police, she said she had felt hair on his chest. . . . [That] troubled detective Woodhouse, because when Davis was providing a blood sample, Woodhouse had seen him shirtless, and Davis's chest was hairless. But in no state in the country can a conviction for rape be based on the fact that both the assailant and the accused have hairy chests. The police knew that they needed more to develop a case against Ritter, and they turned to the possibility of a DNA match.[19]

The FBI forensics lab in Washington, DC, did the DNA analysis. Woodhouse was not surprised when Ritter's DNA matched the DNA taken at the crime scene. Yet even in the face of this conclusive evidence, Carol Sanders continued to insist that Davis, not Ritter, had raped her. Nevertheless, the judge found Ritter guilty and sentenced him to forty years in jail. Had it not been for the existence of DNA profiling technology, Levy points out, Davis, an innocent man, would almost certainly have been the one serving forty years. "It is hard to imagine," Levy says, "a jury acquitting a defendant in a brutal rape when his former girlfriend claims that she . . . recognized him."[20]

Solving Cold Cases

In both the Quintanilla and Ritter cases, DNA evidence convicted these attackers within a few months or a year or two of their committing the crimes. However, two facts—that DNA can last a long time and that forensics labs freeze DNA samples for future reference—allow for solving crimes many years after they occur. In this way, police are able to reopen and solve more cold cases than they could in the past.

Indeed, like the Rodney J. Crooks case in Cincinnati, many seemingly unsolvable cold cases are now solved thanks to state databases of prison inmates' DNA information. DNA evidence from cold crimes can then be compared to these prisoners' DNA profiles. Some states boast extremely encouraging results. In Texas, for example, Gary Stone, an officer in the Texas Department of Public Safety, reports: "We are having some phenomenal results on cases that would have never been solved and people who would have never been arrested. It is unbelievable how far we've come, but also how far we can go."[21]

Law enforcement officials in the state of Washington have also scored successes using DNA to solve cold cases in recent years. One of the most stunning was that of a young rock singer named Mia Zapata, who was raped and murdered in

Different light analysis can show traces of blood or saliva on a victim's body or clothing. Saliva samples found on the chest of singer Mia Zapata helped convict her murderer.

Seattle in 1993. Police investigators were at first baffled by the crime. The only evidence they were able to find consisted of some small drops of saliva on Zapata's chest. The sample was too small to analyze with the RFLP method, at the time the only DNA test available to the local forensics lab. As a result, months and years went by and the case grew colder and colder. At one point, the victim's disappointed father, Richard Zapata, remarked, "I could live and die, and this murder could remain unsolved."[22]

But the steady advance of DNA profiling technology finally broke the case. In 2002, the saliva found at the murder scene was analyzed using PCR and STR at the Washington State Crime Lab. The experts at the lab then entered the profile into the FBI DNA database in hopes of finding a match. And they quickly found one. The suspect DNA belonged to a Cuban immigrant named Jesus Mezquia, then living in Florida. Mezquia was arrested and stood trial in Washington, where he was convicted and sentenced to thirty-six years in prison.

People Freed by DNA Evidence

Whether DNA evidence identifies a criminal quickly or many years after the crime has been committed, convictions obtained this way tell only half the tale of the role DNA profiling plays in criminal justice. The technology has also exonerated many people who had been convicted and jailed for crimes they did not commit. Of these cases, few have been more riveting that of Gary Dotson. A resident of Chicago's suburbs, Dotson was the second American and first person in Illinois ever exonerated by DNA evidence.

Dotson's personal nightmare began in July 1977, when he was 22. On July 9, a 16-year-old girl named Cathleen Crowell told police that she had just been abducted and raped. Three young men had forced her into their car, she said, and one had brutally raped her in the back seat. "I tried to fight him off," she later testified, "and I couldn't."[23] Crowell aided a police artist in preparing a sketch of the alleged rapist. And soon

afterward, she positively identified Dotson, both from his picture in a mug book (a collection of photos of criminal suspects) and in a lineup. Dotson insisted that he was not guilty. Also, at the time of his arrest he had a mustache that he could not have grown in less than a month. Despite the fact that Crowell's sketch was of a clean-shaven man, the authorities ignored this piece of evidence and charged Dotson with the crime. He was tried, found guilty, and received two sentences: 25 to 50 years for rape and 25 to 50 years for kidnapping.

Later, Crowell got married and moved to New Hampshire. One day in 1985, in church, she told her pastor that she was wracked with guilt. When he asked why, she told him that years before, she had falsely accused a man of rape and that the man was still suffering in prison. Crowell explained that back in 1977 she was worried that she might be pregnant by her boyfriend and was afraid that her parents might punish her. So she made up the rape charge. Furthermore, even when she found that she was not pregnant, she continued to lie.

With Crowell's permission, the pastor told a lawyer what had happened. The lawyer tried to get Dotson released, but the prosecutors who had convicted Dotson refused to consider the plea. It later came out that during the trial, prosecuters, eager

Cathleen Crowell Webb with alleged rapist, Gary Dotson, who was wrongly convicted and jailed based on her eyewitness testimony. Dotson became the second American ever exonerated by DNA evidence.

to score a conviction in the case, had knowingly exaggerated some of the flimsy evidence against Dotson, and they feared that a public exoneration might reveal their misconduct.

Thus, shamefully, it was not until August 1989 that a DNA profile finally cleared Dotson. Dotson's lawyers did not know that such technology existed until 1987, and they had to wage long legal battles before the court approved the test. The DNA analysis proved that he was innocent and that Cathleen Crowell had told her pastor the truth about her false accusation. "It's been twelve long, long grueling years," Dotson told reporters after his exoneration. "I'm relieved it's over. [But] the stigma remains. It's something I have to deal with. I've been referred to as a 'convicted rapist.' Now, at least, I'm no longer 'convicted'."[24]

At Death's Door

Perhaps even more wrenching than cases like Dotson's are those in which the inmates freed by DNA analysis were on death row. In such exonerations, of which there were fifteen in the United States by the end of 2006, the innocent parties would surely have been executed had it not been for the existence of DNA profiling technology. The first death row inmate in the world exonerated this way was Kirk Bloodsworth of Cambridge, Maryland. His harrowing story has received a great deal of media attention over the years and inspired a popular book by lawyer and novelist Tim Junkin.

In 1984, Bloodsworth, then 24, was accused of raping and killing a 9-year-old girl. The evidence against him was all circumstantial. (Circumstantial evidence consists of several unrelated facts that when taken together may or may not produce a conclusion or theory about a case.) First, he lived and worked in the general vicinity of the crime. Second, two boys said they saw him walking near the crime scene on the day it occurred. The only forensic evidence was a small semen stain on the girl's panties that could not be matched to Bloodsworth because DNA analysis did not yet exist. Still, the jury found

From Death Row Inmate to Death Penalty Activist

Kirk Bloodsworth, who was wrongfully convicted of murder in 1984 and later exonerated by DNA analysis, was profoundly affected by his experience. Washington Post *reporter Susan Levine gives this moving account of Bloodsworth's nightmare and how he turned it into a force for positive change.*

The dream still haunts him, still grabs him in the night and drags him down the long hallway toward his death. He always fights back, kicking at the faceless guards forcing him on, but there is no escape. The metal-studded gas chamber looms. . . . And then . . . Kirk Bloodsworth wakes up, drenched in terror, choking to breathe. "It's a daily struggle," he says. "You're fighting with the fact you went through this." For the longest time, he wouldn't talk about the past. Ignoring it was the way to move on. But these days, his is one of the most prominent voices within the small, exclusive club of death-row exonerees. . . . Bloodsworth addresses legislative committees, legal conferences and university students . . . and argues against capital punishment for the most fundamental of reasons. "As long as there's the possibility—no matter how remote—that an innocent person could be killed," he says, "nobody should be for the death penalty."

Susan Levine, "Maryland Man's Exoneration Didn't End Nightmare," Washington Post Online. http://www.washingtonpost.com/ac2/wp-dyn?pagename=article&node=&contentId=A55556-2003Feb23&notFound=true

him guilty. This was partly because the prosecutors in the case believed he was the murderer and vigorously argued his guilt in court. "The more I got involved in preparing for the case," stated one of the prosecutors, Robert Lazzaro,

> the more convinced I was that we had the right guy. In my mind, he testified and acted consistent with someone who was guilty. He didn't act like someone who was unjustly accused.... I never would have prosecuted a case I didn't believe in.[25]

U.S. Senator Patrick Leahy (left) speaks with Kirk Bloodsworth (center), the first person freed from death row as a result of DNA testing.

But though the prosecution and jury thought Bloodsworth was guilty, he kept insisting he was innocent all through his nine years in prison, two of them on death row.

Fortunately for Bloodsworth, while he languished in jail DNA profiling technology was rapidly coming to the fore in the U.S. criminal justice system. Before the state of Maryland was able to execute him, his lawyer secured him a DNA test. It showed conclusively that his DNA did not match that in

the semen found on the victim. The court immediately released Bloodsworth and the state paid him $330,000 to help make up for his wrongful imprisonment.

As for Bloodsworth's life since his exoneration, he works as a fisherman and also gives lectures across the country promoting various reforms of the justice system. In particular, he urges more use of DNA testing to free people wrongly convicted of crimes. "Did the system work?" he asked one audience.

> **By the Numbers**
>
> # 15:
>
> As of 2006, the number of death row inmates in the U.S. exonerated by DNA evidence.

I was released, but only after eight years, eleven months, and nineteen days, all that time not knowing whether I would be executed. . . . My life has been taken from me and destroyed. I was separated from my family and branded the worst thing possible—a child killer. I cannot put into words what it is like to live under these circumstances. . . . If it can happen to me, it can happen to you. It can happen to your child, your son, your daughter—it can happen to anybody.[26]

Despite his bitterness over his terrible ordeal, Bloodsworth realizes that in a way he was fortunate. He received his DNA test in time to preserve his life. In marked contrast was the case of a Florida man, Frank Lee Smith. Smith spent fourteen years on death row for a murder he said he did not commit. His lawyers asked repeatedly that he be allowed to have a DNA test, but state prosecutors stubbornly blocked it. Smith finally had his DNA analyzed in 2000 and the results showed he was innocent. But it was too late. He died of cancer in prison before the state could release him. Bloodsworth and other advocates of DNA testing say they do not want to see any more cases like Smith's. They argue that the technology must not only be used to find the truth in criminal cases, it must be used with all possible speed.

CHAPTER 4

Solving Mysteries of the Past and Present

Catching and convicting criminals and freeing falsely imprisoned people are among the most common and important uses for DNA testing techniques. And these were certainly the main uses for DNA testing and analysis in its early days. However, today DNA-related technology is also employed in many other ways, some of them quite ingenious and each important in one way or another to science, society, and/or historians.

Society benefits, for example, when DNA profiling reunites missing children with their families. Similarly, families gain emotional relief and closure when DNA tests prove that years-old human remains are those of a long-lost relative. DNA analysis can also aid scientists in tracing migration patterns of human groups over the course of centuries and millennia. Indeed, studies of ancient DNA are actually beginning to reveal the origins of the human race. In addition, historians benefit from DNA analysis by studying the remains of long dead historical figures and confirming or disproving how certain key historical deaths and other events occurred.

Finally, DNA technology is increasingly used to study and maintain the integrity and balance of the animal kingdom. Some endangered species have already benefited from knowledge gained by studying their DNA. Thus, understanding and analyzing DNA has become a potent tool for unlocking many mysteries of nature and humanity, both in the past and present.

Finding Missing Children

Of the many services DNA analysis has come to provide for society, perhaps none is more gratifying and rewarding than reuniting missing children with their families. The most famous case of using DNA forensics in this manner is that of a group of children in Argentina. In the 1970s, a brutal dictatorial regime gained control of that South American country. In an effort to maintain order by spreading fear, leaders of the regime ordered many innocent people to be killed, tortured, or kidnapped. In the process, about 220 babies were abducted from their families and secretly given to high members of the military to raise as their own.

Uruguayan Sara Mendez spent nearly 25 years searching for her son who had been snatched away by a group of soldiers. DNA forensics has been used in many countries to reunite missing children with their families.

The search for these missing children began when democracy was restored in Argentina in 1983. But for a long time these efforts met with very little success. This situation changed dramatically, however, when reliable DNA profiling technology became available in the 1990s. Since that time, human rights groups and other researchers have sponsored many DNA tests. And so far nearly sixty of the missing children (now young adults) have been found. Of these, about thirty have been reunited with their biological families, while a few have elected to stay with their adoptive families. Seven of the children identified through DNA tests had died in the intervening years.

Among those aiding in the ongoing search in Argentina is Dr. Charles Brenner, a mathematician who aids scientists in performing DNA analysis, especially in finding missing children. In an interview conducted in 2000, Brenner told about one missing child case he helped crack:

> A couple of weeks ago, I got the case of a [prominent elderly resident of Uruguay] named Juan Gelman. His son and daughter-in-law fled to Argentina from Uruguay in the 1970s, and they were killed there as "terrorists." Their little child was apparently auctioned off to someone in the military. Through underground sources, Gelman was eventually able to find out what happened to his grandchild. He was pretty sure a certain young Argentine girl from a military family was her. The girl already had her own suspicions because her adoptive father, on his deathbed, said, "I hope you can forgive me," though he didn't say more. Gelman contacted the girl and . . . my job was to make the calculation [with the aid of DNA analysis] that nailed it down. . . . The data was overwhelmingly consistent that this girl was his grandchild.[27]

Similar efforts to find missing children are ongoing in other countries, notably China. There the Ministry of Public Security has created a DNA database and launched a nationwide campaign to conduct tens of thousands of DNA tests. The goal is to find thousands of children and young women who are abducted each year and sold into slavery or other forms of servitude in various countries. So far the project has found almost five hundred of the missing and reunited them with their families.

Identifying Human Remains

Efforts in Argentina, China, and elsewhere focus mostly on using DNA technology to track down living persons. But DNA analysis is also routinely employed to identify bodies and other human remains. These remains may or may not be related to a crime.

Investigators use conveyor belts to look for human bones and other small remains on the pig farm of alleged serial killer Robert Pickton in 2002.

POLICE LINE DO NOT CROS

Without DNA, often all crimi-
nologists could use to identify a
body would be skeletal remains
and dental records, which don't
provide as definite a match as
DNA.

A gruesome and widely publicized example of DNA identification of unknown murder victims occurred in 2002. Police arrested a serial killer, Robert W. Pickton, a pig farmer in the Canadian province of British Columbia. Pickton admitted to killing at least forty-nine women, many of them prostitutes and drug addicts. Extensive digging at his farm revealed numerous bodies in varying states of decay. Because the police did not know the identity of many of these bodies at first, it was necessary to use DNA profiling to reveal who they were.

There are also many examples of using DNA analysis to identify the remains of people who died of natural causes, in accidents, or in wars. For example, sometimes people get lost in forests or other remote areas and eventually die before they find their way out. Other people are killed in wars or natural disasters and their remains are not found for a long time. When their remains *are* eventually found, DNA tests can very often confirm their identity, almost always to the relief of loved ones.

By the Numbers

A FEW HUNDRED:

As revealed by DNA analysis, the number of early humans that migrated from Africa and gave rise to all modern humans.

Such was the case of U.S. Army soldier Jimmie Dorser, who died at age 18 in combat in the Korean War in 1950. For more than half a century, Dorser was listed as missing in action. In 2002, however, his remains were discovered on a North Korean farm and arrangements were made to ship them to a U.S. Army facility in Hawaii. At the time, though military officials suspected the remains were Dorser's, the identity of the long dead soldier was still uncertain. It was clear to Army forensics experts that only DNA analysis would provide an absolutely positive identification. To that end, surviving members of Dorser's family submitted blood samples so that their DNA could be compared to the DNA found in the remains. "Without that DNA," remarked an Army spokesman, "all they would have gone by was the skeletal remains and the dental records. Those two by themselves aren't bad ways [to identify a body], but they're not going to give you 100 percent [certainty, like DNA can]."[28]

A similar case of DNA analysis identifying an unknown soldier occurred in 1998. Michael Blassie, a 24-year-old U.S. Air Force lieutenant, died in the Vietnam War in 1972, and no one was able to identify his remains. In 1984, these remains were interred in the Tomb of the Unknowns in Arlington National Cemetery in Washington, DC. As the years passed, DNA technology rapidly advanced. In June 1998 the remains were tested and the DNA profile proved they were Blassie's. His family was finally able to give him a proper funeral.

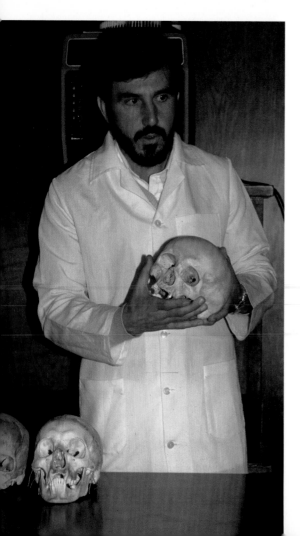

Dr. Daniel Romero Munoz presents forensic evidence identifying an ex-humed skeleton as Nazi war criminal Josef Mengele.

DNA analysis has also been instrumental in identifying human remains from accidents and disasters. A memorable example is the case of one of the victims of the *Titanic*, the famous passenger ship that sunk in the North Atlantic in 1912. Nearly 1500 people lost their lives, and many of the bodies were never found. One body that *was* found was that of a 2-year-old boy pulled from the icy waters by sailors on one of the rescue ships that hurried to the scene of the disaster. The child could not be identified, so he was buried in a mass grave in Nova Scotia along with several other unknown victims of the sinking. Almost a century later, in 2001, local authorities obtained permission to open the grave and perform a DNA test on the boy's remains. The test showed that he was Eino Panula, part of a Finnish family on its way to settle in Pennsylvania. No one in the family survived the disaster.

But thanks to DNA technology, the child's remains were finally returned to his relatives in Finland.

Not all of the deceased individuals identified by DNA testing have elicited the outpourings of sympathy accorded to Dorser, Blassie, Panula, and their families. On occasion, DNA analysis confirms the identity of someone widely detested. So it was in the case of Nazi doctor and war criminal Josef Mengele. During World War II, Mengele became notorious for performing inhumane medical experiments on living prisoners in the Nazi death camp at Auschwitz. After Germany's defeat in the war, Mengele fled to Argentina and later moved to Paraguay and finally Brazil. He reportedly died in a drowning accident in Brazil in 1979. However, many people remained suspicious that this might be a cover story and that he might still be alive. Ironically, in the end, science, originally Mengele's chosen profession, revealed the true identity of a human monster. A DNA test performed on the body from the drowning showed that the remains were his indeed.

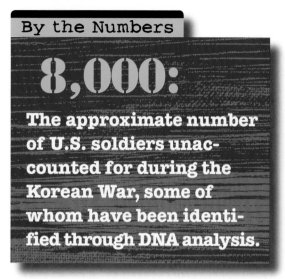

By the Numbers

8,000: The approximate number of U.S. soldiers unaccounted for during the Korean War, some of whom have been identified through DNA analysis.

The Fate of Long Dead Royals Revealed

The human remains described so far all came from people who lived and died in the past century. But in some cases it is possible to perform DNA tests on remains that are centuries old. When enough viable DNA is recovered from such remains, modern scientists can shed light on well-known historical personalities and events, in some cases including infamous crimes, injustices, and/or mishaps of the past. Using DNA analysis and other forensic methods to study the remains of long-dead people is the work of specially trained scientists known as forensic anthropologists.

Forensic anthropologists use DNA analysis and other methods to study the remains of long-dead people.

Forensic anthropologists were among the experts who solved one of Europe's greatest historical mysteries in 2000. That riddle, which had haunted generations of French, involved the fate of Louis-Charles, the young son of King Louis XVI and his wife Marie Antoinette. Their monarchy had been overthrown during the French Revolution, which had erupted in 1789. On January 21, 1793, King Louis was executed. Marie Antoinette met the same fate later that year. That left their 8-year-old son, Louis-Charles, as their heir, and some of his royal relatives promptly dubbed him King Louis XVII. This was unofficial and ultimately meaningless, since the child was in custody and had no real power.

The question was: What happened to the boy? The official version released by members of the revolutionary government was that Louis-Charles spent two years in a windowless cell in a drab Paris prison before dying of tuberculosis in June 1795 at age 10. However, many people in France and elsewhere did not believe this claim, viewing it as a devious cover story concocted by the government. As Australian geneticist Anna Meyer tells it:

> Almost immediately, people began to whisper that Louis-Charles was not dead—that the prince had been exchanged at some earlier time for another child, who had died in his place. The real Louis XVII was now hidden somewhere, most likely away from France. There was absolutely no proof that the child who died was the genuine Louis-Charles. . . . Even the warders who had guarded him could neither confirm nor deny whether the child who died was the real Louis XVII. . . . To add to the mystery, no one who knew him as a young child, not even his sister, had been permitted to identify the body.[29]

Thus, for nearly two centuries historians and others argued over whether Louis-Charles had died in prison or had survived into adulthood. Finally, in the 1990s various interested parties proposed using the recently introduced DNA profiling technology to settle this argument. To do so, of course, they needed a DNA sample from the child who died in the Paris prison. They also needed a DNA sample from someone related to the French royal family for comparison. No closely related descendants could be found. But fortunately a set of rosary beads belonging to Marie Antoinette's mother had survived, and some medallions intertwined with the beads contained locks of hair belonging to Louis-Charles's aunts and uncles.

As for the sample from the imprisoned boy, it so happened that after his death a doctor had removed and saved his heart in a jar. Modern investigators managed to find the heart. Then forensic anthropologists went to work and were able to confirm conclusively that the boy who died in the prison was indeed the crown prince. Thanks to DNA analysis, the mystery had at last been solved.

Forensic anthropologists solved another mystery involving European royals in 1994. In this case, the mystery involved the fate of Russia's last Czar (supreme monarch), Nicholas II. Not long after the start of the Russian Revolution in 1917, some of the revolutionaries placed Nicholas, his wife, and five children under house arrest. Later, in June 1918, all seven members of the royal family disappeared without a trace. Rumors claimed that a firing squad had executed them and buried their bodies in a mass grave.

Many years went by. Then, in 1989 a grave with several skeletons was discovered near the house in which the Russian royals were staying at the time of their disappearance. But were

The Czar's Unusual DNA

When modern researchers examined the supposed remains of the last Russian Czar, Nicholas II, the first DNA test they performed was inconclusive. The investigators managed to find two living descendants of the Romanovs, the royal family to which Nicholas belonged. They compared the mitochondrial DNA (mtDNA) from these relatives to the mtDNA found in the decades-old remains. Though the genetic material in all three samples was very similar, the mtDNA from the remains did not exactly match that from the living relatives. The researchers suspected that Nicholas had a very rare condition known as heteroplasmy. People with this condition have some odd sequences in some parts of their DNA. To test this theory, the investigators obtained permission to exhume (dig up) the body of Nicholas's brother, Georgij Romanov. Sure enough, Georgij's mtDNA had the same odd heteroplasmy markers as Nicholas's did. The perfect match showed that the remains were indeed those of Nicholas and that the heteroplasmy had disappeared in later generations of Romanovs.

these truly the remains of Nicholas and his family? Various forensic tests were conducted, culminating with DNA profiles. These tests proved that the bones did belong to the murdered royals. Another historical mystery had been solved by DNA technology.

Unraveling the Mysteries of Human Origins

The same technology promises to solve far older historical mysteries as well. Because DNA can, under favorable circumstances, last for many thousands of years, DNA analysis is beginning to reveal secrets about Stone Age humans, their migrations, and even their origins.

There was much speculation about the death of Russia's last Czar, Nicholas II, until forensic tests proved that his were among remains found in a mass grave.

For example, recent studies of the DNA of modern humans suggest that all people alive today, regardless of skin color, are, genetically speaking, nearly identical. Among other things, these studies looked at average rates of mutations (natural changes) in the human genome and traced these changes backward in time. The studies, Meyer explains, found

> the startling fact that all humans, whether from Asia, Africa, or Europe, or anywhere else for that mater, have astonishingly *similar* DNA. . . . This implied that modern-day humans are all very closely related, and therefore likely to have a had a very recent common ancestor.[30]

This analysis of modern human DNA indicates that a common ancestor lived sometime between 140,000 and 290,000 years ago. That ancestor was one of a small group of early humans who were descended from still more primitive humans. Moreover, the same studies suggest that this common human ancestral group originated in Africa.

Separate studies of ancient human DNA uncovered in Malaysia in the last few years confirm these findings. A team of geneticists headed by Dr. Vincent Macaulay of the University of Glasgow also found that all people alive today are descended from a single group of early humans. That group, consisting of perhaps no more than a few hundred people, moved out of Africa about 65 thousand years ago. Over the centuries, their descendants migrated eastward through what are now the Middle East, India, and Southeast Asia. They reached Australia by about 50 thousand years ago.

A Neanderthal skull, left, and a Cro-Magnon skull. Timeframes discovered by DNA studies have proven that Neanderthals and Cro-Magnons were unrelated and evolved separately.

Based on the tale told by the ancient DNA, Macaulay and his colleagues think that human settlement of Europe occurred a few thousand years later. Science writer Nicholas Wade reported the team's findings:

> Because these events occurred in the last Ice Age, when Europe was at first too cold for human habitation . . . it was populated only later, not directly from Africa but as an offshoot of the southern migration. [Some members] of this offshoot would presumably have trekked back through the lands that are now India and Iran to reach the [Middle] East and Europe.[31]

Similar studies of ancient human DNA have settled arguments over possible kinship between these modern-like humans who originated in Africa and another group of early humans—the Neanderthals. Skeletons of Neanderthals, who had stocky bodies, heavy jaws, and thick eyebrow ridges, began to come to light in the 1850s. To date, the remains of almost five hundred individual Neanderthals have been found at some eighty sites in Europe and the Middle East. DNA extracted from some of these remains is between 29 thousand and 42 thousand years old. Scientists have also unearthed DNA from modern-style humans (often called Cro-Magnons) in caves in Italy. This DNA, dating from 23 thousand to 25 thousand years ago, does not match the Neanderthal DNA. As a result, the current scientific consensus is that the Neanderthals and Cro-Magnons were unrelated and evolved separately. "In a stunning example of the power of ancient DNA research," Meyer says,

> the Neanderthal DNA work has finally made it possible, after 150 years of debate, to say with some certainty that the enigmatic [mysterious] Neanderthals are not the ancestors of humans, but are simply an example of an extinct species, [although] an extremely interesting one.[32]

Identifying lost soldiers, unraveling historical mysteries, and searching for humanity's origins are only a few of the many ingenious uses devised for DNA technology in recent years. Experts agree that the technology is still in its infancy. So it is likely that future uses will be developed that people today have not yet imagined.

Neanderthal DNA Not a Match

In her book The DNA Detectives, Anna Meyer gives this account of what modern scientists found when they analyzed DNA from Neanderthal bones tens of thousands of years old and compared them to modern human DNA.

No one could have been in any doubt that the task of extracting and analyzing Neanderthal DNA would be one of the most challenging ancient DNA projects ever attempted. So Neanderthal researchers decided to approach one of the pioneers of ancient DNA research, Svante Pääbo, from the Zoological Institute at the University of Munich, in Germany. . . . Pääbo removed a tiny 3.5 g [0.12 ounce] sample of bone from the right humerus [leg bone] of a Neanderthal. . . . When Pääbo [extracted and examined] the sequence of Neanderthal DNA with the sequence from the equivalent section of modern human DNA, there was no mistaking the results. Neanderthal DNA and human DNA were quite different. To be exact, Pääbo . . . found that the Neanderthal DNA varied from human DNA sequences by an average of 26 individual differences.

Anna Meyer, The DNA Detectives. New York: Thunder Mouth, 2005, pp. 29-31.

CHAPTER 5

Legal and Ethical Issues of DNA Testing

No one argues that DNA profiling technology has not revolutionized the criminal justice system in recent years. In large numbers of crime investigations, DNA testing has been pivotal in finding and convicting the culprits. Moreover, hundreds of people mistakenly convicted of crimes have been freed. In addition, the creation of DNA computer databases has made cracking cold cases easier and enhanced the ability to identify unknown human remains.

However, some individuals and groups have expressed concerns over various aspects of the new technology. They agree that DNA analysis has been a boon in certain ways. Yet they worry that, like any other powerful technology, it has the potential for misuse and/or unintended negative consequences.

Invasions of Privacy?

Among these potential negative consequences, perhaps the most widely debated issue is personal privacy. A number of critics say that DNA testing is already being used to invade people's privacy through its ability to reveal intimate details about them. Robin McKie, of the online newspaper *Guardian Unlimited*, sums it up this way:

> Once it was possible to lead a discreet, anonymous life. [But] now our movements can be laid bare by forensic genetics, a power that has already affected millions of people, including criminals, suspects, policemen, immigrants, parents, offspring, and lawyers. It has even become the subject of TV voyeurism, with teenage fathers being told on live TV whether or not they are

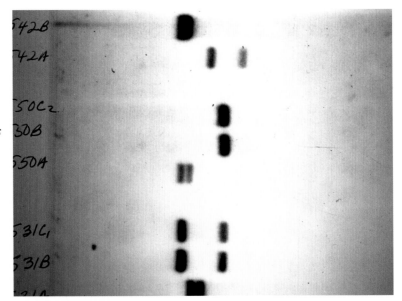

This human DNA fingerprint taken from blood can reveal intimate aspects about a person's life and health. Many critics are concerned that insurance companies can misuse information obtained from DNA testing to discriminate against clients.

the biological fathers of their partners' babies. And in the future, as the technique's power is enhanced even further, [DNA] samples [may] provide not just names but information about suspects' race, hair color, and facial features.[33]

This fear of the power of genetic fingerprinting to intrude into and lay bare people's personal lives is not limited to members of the media or any other single societal group. It is shared by people of all walks of life, including the scientists who developed and/or continue to use the technology. For example, researchers at the Human Genome Project (an effort by the U.S. Department of Energy and the National Institutes of Health to map the human genome) state in their official Web site:

DNA can provide insights into many intimate aspects of a person and their families including susceptibility to particular diseases, legitimacy of birth, and perhaps predispositions to certain behaviors and sexual orientation. This increases the potential for genetic discrimination by government, insurers, employers, schools, banks, and others.[34]

Of these potential discriminators, insurers have frequently been singled out in recent years. Many critics say that insurance companies have particularly strong incentives

Discrimination in Hiring

One of the concerns voiced in recent years about increasingly large DNA databases is that information from these systems might be secretly sold to outside parties. These parties might include employers who want to practice discrimination in hiring. This concern is concisely summed up by the Council for Responsible Genetics, based in Cambridge, Massachusetts:

Basing employment decisions on genetic status opens the door to unfounded generalizations about employee performance and increases acceptance of the notion that employers need to exercise such discrimination in order to lower labor costs. . . . [Many] employers face economic pressures to identify workers who are likely to remain healthy. Less absenteeism, reduced life and health insurance costs, and longer returns on investments in employee training all reduce the costs of labor. To the extent that employers believe that genetic information can help identify workers who have a "healthy constitution," they have strong economic incentives to screen applicants and workers. Such policies victimize all workers. Discrimination against individuals with particular genetic characteristics harms all workers by diverting attention from the need to improve and, if possible, eliminate workplace and environmental conditions that contribute to ill health for everyone.

Council for Responsible Genetics, "Genetic Discrimination."
http://www.gene-watch.org/programs/privacy/genetic-disc-position.html
Development of DNA Profiling

for possible misuse of information obtained through DNA testing. The fear is that some of these companies may discriminate against clients whose DNA profiles show that they have a high likelihood of developing serious health problems later. This, critics say, would significantly reduce costs for insurers. At the same time, it would raise both legal and ethical red flags, raising questions about possible infringements on a client's civil rights. According to the Council for Responsible Genetics, a nonprofit organization located in Cambridge, Massachusetts:

Individuals can exercise choices about whether to smoke, how much exercise they get, and how much fat is in their diets. [But] they cannot change the contents of their genes. To make employment or insurance decisions on the basis of genetic characteristics determined at the moment of conception is to discard cherished beliefs in justice and equality.[35]

Similar worries have been voiced about the potential for employers, police organizations, government agencies, and other individuals or groups to misuse DNA information. These worries have led to debates among lawmakers on local, state, and federal levels. And in fact, several U.S. states have already passed legislation that prohibits insurance companies, the police, employers, and others from some types of genetic discrimination. The most sweeping version was that enacted by Massachusetts in 2000. Since that time, more than thirty other states have passed laws banning various kinds of misuse of DNA information. Experts expect all states to have such laws within a few years.

Worries About Racial Profiling

Another privacy-related issue related to DNA testing is racial profiling and the possible use of such racial information to discriminate. At present, DNA analysis lacks the ability to identify certain physical characteristics such as skin color. However, the technology can be used to trace a person's ancestry. So if a

DNA Profiling's Inventor Voices Concerns

In an interview conducted in August 2004 with the online journal Guardian Unlimited, Alec Jeffreys, the inventor of DNA profiling stated several of his concerns about the legal and ethical implications of rapidly advancing DNA profiling technology.

Imagine DNA details about racial groups falling into the hands of some governments or [private] organizations. It is not a pleasant prospect.... Today unscrupulous investigators can easily get your DNA profile—from saliva on a coffee cup or cigarette butt—and then use it to show whether you are the "real" parent of your child. It's illegal but simple to do, and I am very sure it occurs quite often. It is a gross invasion of a person's privacy.... If [the] scientists [working on ways to make DNA profiling determine a person's race] are successful they will provide police with the means of working out people's racial and medical histories just from the DNA they leave behind. That is just not [right].

Guardian Unlimited Online, "Meet the DNA Genius Who Fears the Dark Side of his Discovery."
http://www.guardian.co.uk/genes/article/0,2763,1278710,00.html

DNA sample taken from a crime scene reveals African ancestry, it might mean that the suspect has dark skin (although he or she might just as well have light skin).

One worry is that, however accurate or inaccurate such racial profiling may be, it might be used to intimidate or persecute an entire racial or ethnic community. Such fears surfaced in Charlottesville, Virginia, in 2003, for example. A serial rapist had been terrorizing the area for several years. One eyewitness said the culprit appeared to be an African American. The local police finally decided to canvas local African American males and ask them for DNA samples, a move that ignited both controversy and protests. According to one observer, many in the local African American community "saw the DNA sweep, or dragnet, as a form of racial profiling, and an invasion of civil liberties."[36]

Local police have enforced DNA sweeps of areas, taking samples from a large number of people, based not on evidence but general suspicion. Many feel that this is a form of racial profiling and an invasion of civil liberties.

Eddie Joe Lloyd, right, was exonerated with DNA evidence after spending 17 years in prison. The Innocence Project is an organization dedicated to using DNA testing to free mistakenly convicted people.

Nevertheless, more than one hundred African American men in Charlottesville volunteered their DNA in the sweep. Many of them later said that they did so because they felt pressured. This raised another related legal and privacy issue: whether asking for DNA samples from people who are not suspects in a crime can be interpreted as a type of coercion, or intimidation. In other words, a person might fear that refusing to give a sample might make him or her a suspect and so feel forced to provide the sample. One of the men canvassed in the Charlottesville sweep complained:

They kept asking, they kept asking. They said 'since you will not provide a sample, we are going to come to your classes, sit in on them, [and] make sure you really are a student here.' I think they're harassing people, they're intimidating people. I think they're obtaining DNA under duress.[37]

This potential abuse of DNA profiling information has been concisely summed up by noted attorney Barry Scheck, director of the Innocence Project, an organization dedicated to using DNA testing to exonerate mistakenly convicted people. "It's inherently coercive," Scheck contends, "when a policeman comes to your door and says, 'Give us a sample of your blood and if you don't give it to us, you're a suspect.'"[38]

The police who conduct such DNA sweeps often counter that their motive is not to harass, but rather simply to catch a criminal. Sometimes, they say, such sweeps are the only means they have of narrowing the search. For instance, Charlottesville's police chief gave the following response to charges of DNA racial profiling:

Anything we do in law enforcement is a balance. On one side of the balance scale is [the] need to preserve and protect individual rights. And human dignity. On the other side of the balance scale is the need to perform a legitimate law enforcement purpose. In this case it was to apprehend a serial rapist.[39]

Potential Problems With Databases

Another mounting legal and ethical concern involves the relationship between rapidly advancing DNA technology and existing DNA databases. Some people worry that technological advances will sooner or later make these databases obsolete, or at least less efficient. When that happens, the critics warn, it could create legal challenges to DNA profile matches obtained from such systems. Even the inventor of DNA analysis, Alec Jeffreys, has expressed concerns about outmoded databases. "To pretend that we've gone from [the system I introduced] to the ultimate DNA typing system is nonsense," he asserts.

There'll be other ones coming along [even more advanced than PCR and STR], and that actually creates a major problem for the forensic scientist who is interested in databasing, because once you go in for very large-scale databasing of many thousands of people—you are trapped in that technology. You cannot change that technology because you've got to retype everybody in the database if you do. So the drive towards databasing, I think, is in fundamental conflict with the still rapidly evolving field of forensic DNA typing—the technology itself.[40]

Large databases are often used to store DNA testing information. However, there is concern about the ability of existing DNA databases to adapt to, or incorporate, new advances in DNA technology.

DNA testing is still a relatively new technology and is expected to improve as time goes on.

Another potential legal, as well as ethical, problem associated with the use of large DNA databases is illustrated by a widely publicized mistake that occurred in February 2000 in England. A few months before, police in the city of Manchester collected some biological evidence at the site of a burglary. The local forensics lab analyzed the sample using a version of the STR method that recognized six loci, or gene locations (each containing several tandem repeats), on a DNA molecule. The odds of the genetic information in all six loci being identical in two separate individuals were about one in 37 million. They then entered the profile into England's national DNA database, which at the time contained some 660 thousand DNA profiles. Because that number is so much smaller than 37 million, the analysts assumed there would be little chance of a random match. So when a match *was* found, the police promptly arrested the man whose DNA in the database matched that found at the crime scene.

However, the suspect strongly insisted he was innocent. Moreover, he had proof that he was somewhere else when the crime occurred. Nevertheless, based on the strength of the DNA match alone, he was kept in jail for months awaiting trial. Fortunately for him, his attorney demanded that a second, more comprehensive DNA test be performed. This time the analysts compared the genetic information in nine loci rather than six, raising the odds of a random match to one in many billions. And sure enough, the suspect's DNA no longer matched that found at the crime scene. Clearly, the database match had been random and false—the result of what might be termed an "unlucky" coincidence. The culprit and suspect were among a handful of people in the world whose DNA matched in six genetic locations. Only when a higher number of loci were considered did the uniqueness of their individual

Becoming a Forensic DNA Specialist

Job Description:
A Forensic DNA specialist does DNA casework and analysis using the most advanced equipment and techniques available. He or she identifies various biological materials and works with less experienced lab analysts, in some cases supervising them. The forensic DNA special also writes case reports summarizing DNA tests. These reports will be used by prosecutors and other law enforcement officials.

Education:
A DNA specialist usually must have a master's degree in biology, biochemistry, molecular biology, genetics, or a comparable science.

Qualifications:
In addition to a master's degree in a biological science, a DNA specialist is expected to have at least one year of experience doing DNA casework. A strong familiarity with PCR, STR, and other standard DNA lab techniques is a must.

Additional Information:
A DNA specialist is also expected to possess extensive knowledge of DNA databases, including CODIS and laws and procedures relating to rules of evidence in a courtroom. He or she must also have strong organizational abilities and be able to write and speak in public clearly and persuasively. Computer skills are also a must.

Salary:
$45,000-$90,000

DNA profiles become apparent. Forensic DNA experts Rudin and Inman explained the implications and lessons of this now famous case:

> It is not only unsurprising, but expected, that the larger the database, the greater chance of a coincidental match. As databases grow, greater numbers of . . . loci are required to reduce the possibility of an [accidental] hit. . . . Additionally, a profile frequency of one in 37 million does not mean that the six loci cannot match more than one person in 37 million. . . . It does not mean that there cannot be two [such matches], and it also does not exclude the possibility of finding two of the same six-locus profiles in the first 660,000 people tested.[41]

A Technology with a Strong Future

There are two sides to the DNA analysis coin, so to speak. On the one hand, DNA databases must keep up with DNA analysis systems. On the other, those systems must be sensitive enough to keep pace with rapidly expanding databases. These facts make changing DNA profiling technology itself a potential source of ethical arguments and legal disputes, along with privacy, racial profiling, and other issues relating to people's civil rights.

It must be kept in mind, however, that DNA testing is still a relatively new technology, and scientists, police, and lawmakers are still working on how to make it more accurate, reliable, and fair. Because of this, DNA testing is expected to improve as time goes on. "The future of DNA analysis remains strong," attorney Harlan Levy asserts. "It has become more and more like the 'fingerprint' it was initially supposed to be, uniquely identifying an individual. This trend can only be expected to continue."[42]

Notes

Introduction: In the Footsteps of Sherlock Holmes

1. Quoted in E.J. Wagner, *The Science of Sherlock Holmes*. New York: John Wley, 2006, p.8.

2. Quoted in Wagner, *Science of Sherlock Holmes*, p. 8.

3. Quoted in Wagner, *Science of Sherlock Holmes*, p. 150.

4. Robin Franzen, "TV's 'CSI' Crime Drama Makes It Look Too Easy," *Portland Oregonian*, December 10, 2002.

5. Harlan Levy, *And the Blood Cried Out: A Prosecutor's Spellbinding Account of the Power of DNA*. New York: HarperCollins, 1996, p. 199.

Chapter 1: Development of DNA Profiling

6. Levy, *And the Blood Cried Out*, p. 16.

7. Quoted in The Human Genome, "Discovering DNA Fingerprinting." http://genome.wellcome.ac.uk/doc_wtd020877.html" http://genome.wellcome.ac.uk/doc_wtd020877.html.

8. Quoted in Science Watch, "Sir Alec Jeffreys on DNA Profiling." http://www.sciencewatch.com/interviews/sir_alec_jeffreys.htm.

9. Levy, *And the Blood Cried Out*, p. 25.

10. N.E. Genge, *The Forensic Casebook: The Science of Crime Scene Investigation*. New York: Ballantine, 2002, p. 144.

11. Quoted in Forensic Science Service, "Colin Pitchfork-First Murder Conviction on DNA Evidence Also Clears the Prime Suspect." http://www.forensic.gov.uk/forensic_t/inside/news/list_casefiles.php?case=1.

12. Levy, *And the Blood Cried Out*, p. 31.

Chapter 2: How DNA Profiling Works

13. Quoted in Genge, *Forensic Casebook*, p. 146.

14. Genge, Forensic Casebook, p. 149.

15. Norah Rudin and Keith Inman, *An Introduction to Forensic DNA Analysis*. New York: CRC, 2002, p. 16.

16. Genge, *Forensic Casebook*, p. 151.

17. CODIS, "National DNA Index System." http://www.fbi.gov/hq/lab/codis/national.htm.

Chapter 3: Classic Cases of DNA Profiling

18. Court TV News, "Expert: Daughter's DNA Found on Evidence at Murdered Parents' Home." http://www.courttv.com/trials/johnson/021705_ctv.html

19. Levy, *And the Blood Cried Out*, p. 99.

20. Levy, *And the Blood Cried Out*, p. 102.

21. Quoted in "DNA Cracks Cold Cases," *Austin American-Statesman*, July 24, 2005.

22. Quoted in CBS News, "Who Murdered the Rock Star?" http://www.cbsnews.com/stories/2004/05/14/48hours/main617479.shtml.

23. Quoted in Northwestern University School of Law, "The Rape That Wasn't—the First DNA Exoneration in Illinois." http://www.law.northwestern.edu/depts/clinic/wrongful/exonerations/Dotson.htm.

24. Quoted in "The Rape That Wasn't."

25. Quoted in CNN.com, "Kirk Bloodsworth, Twice Convicted of Rape and Murder, Exonerated by DNA Evidence." http://archives.cnn.com/2000/LAW/06/20/bloodsworth.profile.

26. Quoted in Tim Junkin, Bloodsworth: The True Story of the First Death Row Inmate Exonerated by DNA. Chapel Hill, NC: Algonquin, 2004, pp. 268-269.

Chapter 4: Solving Mysteries of the Past and Present

27. Quoted in New York Times on the Web, "A Math Sleuth Whose Secret Weapon Is Statistics." http://dna-view.com/ny-times.htm.

28. Quoted in "Remains of Korean War Soldier Reunited With Family," *Orange County Register,* February 14, 2007.

29. Anna Meyer, *The DNA Detectives*. New York: Thunder Mouth, 2005, p. 179.

30. Meyer, *DNA Detectives*, pp. 26-27.

31. New York Times On Line, "DNA Study Yields Clues on First Migration of Early Humans." http://www.nytimes.com/2005/05/13/science/13migrate.html?ex=1273636800&en=4a3b9de4a84891b7&ei=5090&partner=rssuserland.

32. Meyer, *DNA Detectives*, p. 34.

Chapter 5: Legal and Ethical Issues of DNA Testing

33. Guardian Unlimited, "Meet the DNA Genius Who Fears the Dark Side of his Discovery." http://www.guardian.co.uk/genes/article/0,2763,1278710,00.html.

34. Human Genome Project, "DNA Forensics: Ethical, Legal and Social Concerns." http://www.ornl.gov/sci/techresources/Human_Genome/elsi/forensics.shtml#4.

35. Council for Responsible Genetics, "Genetic Discrimination." http://www.gene-watch.org/programs/privacy/genetic-disc-position.html.

36. Quoted in PBS: Religion and Ethics Newsweekly, "DNA Testing and Crime." http://www.pbs.org/wnet/religionandethics/week739/cover.html.

37. Quoted in "DNA Testing and Crime."

38. Quoted in Nature Genetics, "Forensic Genetics and Ethical, Legal and Social Implications Beyond the Clinic." http://www.nature.com/ng/journal/v36/n11s/full/ng1594.html.

39. Quoted in "DNA Testing and Crime."

40. Quoted in "Sir Alec Jeffreys on DNA Profiling."

41. Rudin and Inman, *Introduction to Forensic DNA Analysis*, p. 173.

42. Levy, *And the Blood Cried Out*, p. 193.

Glossary

allele: Part of or an alternate form of a gene found in a DNA molecule.

base pair: Two complementary chemical bases that together form a rung connecting the two strands making up a DNA double helix.

biological evidence: Cells, hairs, bodily fluids, and other materials derived from living things.

CODIS (Combined DNA Index System): A national DNA database run by the FBI. CODIS coordinates with and stores information from smaller state databases.

DNA (deoxyribonucleic acid): The genetic material making up the blueprint of most life on Earth.

DNA database: A computerized catalogue of DNA profiles.

DNA extraction: A lab procedure in which DNA is removed from the nuclei of cells.

DNA profiling (or DNA analysis or testing): The process of determining the unique genetic markers of a living thing for comparison with others.

double helix: The two-stranded twisting spiral comprising the basic structure of each DNA molecule.

exoneration: Freeing a person wrongly arrested for or convicted of a crime.

forensic anthropologist: A specially trained scientist who uses DNA analysis and other forensic methods to study the remains of long-dead people.

forensic science (or forensics): The application of scientific methods to legal matters, particularly solving crimes.

gene: A piece or section of DNA that contains all the information needed to produce a single genetic trait, such as brown eyes.

heredity: The passing on of physical characteristics and traits from one generation to another through DNA in the cells.

human genome: The total genetic makeup of human beings.

loci (singular, locus): Locations of specific genes within genetic material.

minisatellites: In the DNA molecule, tiny repeating segments that can differ from one person to another.

mitochondrial DNA (mtDNA): DNA found in other parts of a cell rather than the nucleus. Mitochondrial DNA is passed only from mother to child rather than from both parents.

MO (from the Latin modus ope-randi): A method or pattern of behavior employed consistently by a criminal.

mutations: Tiny changes in genetic material caused by copying errors during cell division or by exposure to radiation, chemicals, viruses, or other outside agents.

nucleus (plural, nuclei): The central portion of an animal or plant cell.

PCR (polymerase chain reaction): A lab process that uses a chemical to create extra copies of the DNA molecules in a biological sample.

prosecutor: In the criminal justice system, a lawyer charged by a local, state, or federal government with convicting a suspected criminal.

RFLP (restriction fragment length polymorphism): A DNA analysis system that probes, cuts, and sorts DNA fragments of varying lengths and then takes a snapshot of them using an X-ray machine.

STR (short tandem repeat): A DNA analysis system that examines repeated short sequences in the base pairs of the DNA double helix.

For More Information

Books

William Hunter, *DNA Analysis*. Philadelphia: Mason Crest, 2006. A well-written introduction to DNA profiling and how it helps solve crimes.

Tim Junkin, *Bloodsworth: The True Story of the First Death Row Inmate Exonerated by DNA*. Chapel Hill, NC: Algonquin, 2004. Tells Kirk Bloodsworth's riveting story in detail. Recommended for advanced young readers.

Anna Meyer, *The DNA Detectives.* New York: Thunder Mouth, 2005. A fascinating exploration of how DNA profiling can be used to solve mysteries of the past, including what happened to France's King Louis XVII.

Kenneth G. Rainis, *Blood and DNA Evidence: Crime-Solving Science Experiments.* Berkeley Heights, NJ: Enslow, 2006. Written for basic readers, this book effectively explains how forensic scientists use blood and DNA evidence to solve crimes.

Diane Yancey, *Murder.* Farmington Hills, MI: Lucent, 2006. Explains how forensics helps solve murder cases using various kinds of crime scene evidence, including DNA traces.

Internet

How Stuff Works, "How Crime Scene Investigation Works: Analyzing the Evidence." http://science.howstuff-works.com/csi5.htm. A short but effective overview of the subject, with a fascinating section comparing real CSI investigations to the ones depicted on television.

International Crime Scene Investigators Association, "How to Become a CSI." http://www.icsia.org/faq.html. Tells in detail how to pursue a career in crime scene investigation.

National Public Radio, Interview with Sir Alec Jeffries. http://www.npr.org/templates/story/story.php?storyId=4756341. Contains a link to an audio recording of an interview with the British researcher who introduced DNA fingerprinting in the 1980s.

Index

Picture Credits

About the Author

In addition to his numerous acclaimed volumes on ancient civilizations, historian Don Nardo has published several studies of modern scientific and medical discoveries and phenomena. Among these are *Germs, Atoms, Biological Warfare, Eating Disorders, Breast Cancer, Vaccines, Malnutrition,* and biographies of scientists Charles Darwin and Tycho Brahe. Mr. Nardo lives with his wife Christine in Massachusetts.